BREAD
ON THE
TABLE

BREAD
ON THE
TABLE

THE STORY OF LOTTIE PORTER
AND THE FAMILY SHE RAISED

Renetta Burlage

CAMPANILE
PUBLISHING

Bread on the Table

Copyright © 2009 by Renetta Burlage

Cover design illustrated by Scott Nychay - www.nychay.com

CAMPANILE
PUBLISHING

Campanile Publishing LLC, Iowa, USA -
www.campanilepublishing.com

ISBN: 978-0-9823759-1-4

To my Mother, Helene Porter Salemink:
Thank you for sharing your memories.

ACKNOWLEDGMENTS

To Mother: Your daily reminders of your life at home with Grandma will not be forgotten. Thank you for sharing your memories and stories of the hard times and the good times. You inspired me to write them down and I hope they will live on for future generations.

To Michael: Your encouragement, love and support helped me to realize my dream of becoming a writer. Thank you for helping out with the kids and for stepping in when needed. Thank you, too, for always keeping me grounded.

To Sara: Thank you for your patience and understanding and for giving Mom the space and time needed to write.

To Luke: Thank you for your thoughtfulness and visits to my office when I was writing. You, too, were very patient.

To my parents and family: Thank you for your encouragement and support. I hope I have given something back by writing down our family history.

To my aunts and uncles: Thank you for sharing your memories. I will never grow tired of hearing your family stories.

To my dear friend, Baylissa: You inspired me to write and have taught me so much about life and living. Thank you for your constant encouragement, wisdom, love and support.

To Grandma Porter: I will always marvel at the strength and courage you had when faced with difficult times. Thank you for passing on your remarkable spirit.

Lottie Porter 1943

CONTENTS

Preface 1

Sandy Days and Sandy Times 5

Living on "Sand 60".. 23

Watermelon Days 43

Our Daily Bread..61

A New Farm..77

A Change in the Wind... 83

Mother's Strength... 95

We Are Family 107

Holding It Together... 117

Family Ties and New Beginnings..................................... 131

Epilogue...141

PREFACE

WHILE GROWING UP, it seemed as though not a day passed by without my mother repeating a phrase that Grandma Porter would typically say. We commonly heard stories about our mother's childhood, growing up on a sandy farm with her brothers and sisters. These were memories shared from times of the Great Depression. However, having lived for years on a meager income, the Great Depression was not felt as much in their lives as it may have been elsewhere. Every day was a struggle, but as long as food was put on the table, there was little to complain about and much to be grateful for.

My grandma, Lottie DeVault Ulch Porter was born in Solon, Iowa in 1894. She attended country school in Solon and later married Frank Ulch in 1913. They farmed near Solon and had two sons, Ardell and Lee. Following Frank Ulch's untimely death, Lottie met her future husband, James Porter, on a train ride back from Olathe, Kansas to visit her aunt. They were married in 1921 and settled in a house in Conesville, Iowa. Lottie and James Porter had seven children: Raymond, Ronald John, Mary Jane, Warren, Jeanne, Helene and Jim. Ardell and Lee, and James Porter's son, Willy, completed the family.

The following is an account of Lottie's life while raising her family during these uncertain times. Her incredible strength and courage were evident in her daily plight to provide for her family while often faced with adversity. However, the family was very close and the way in which they bonded and respected each other was admirable, thereby making good times and lasting memories amongst each other.

So much can be learned from history, especially the historical significance gained from one's own family. It has been my pleasure to research and write this book, gleaning insight from the notes and interviews I have had with my mother, aunts and uncles. May these memories live on and their story not be forgotten as we pay tribute to the extraordinary life of their mother, Lottie Porter, while observing important, historical moments in American and world history.

1

SANDY DAYS
AND SANDY TIMES

"AT TWO O'CLOCK this afternoon, Charles Lindbergh will be flying his plane, *The Spirit of St. Louis,* over the town of Conesville, Iowa. Be sure to watch the sky to see this famous man in flight." This was the message Mother was given amidst the static when she picked up the receiver, having heard a general ring on the country line telephone. General rings on this multiple party line signaled that it was an important call, such as a weather warning.

Everyone answered at the same time. Today's message, however, was unique and exciting.

It was May 1927 and Charles Lindbergh had recently flown across the Atlantic Ocean in his single-engine plane, *The Spirit of St. Louis*. Now on his way home, he had stopped in St. Paul, Minnesota and would soon be flying over southeast Iowa to reach his destination in St. Louis, Missouri. That afternoon was clear and sunny and Mother, Dad and the boys gathered out in the yard to wait and watch. It was rare to see or hear any plane, but after several minutes passed, at last the faint sound of a buzzing airplane was heard. One of the boys, Lee, climbed up on the roof of the chicken house to get a better view. "Look Dad, it's him, Charles Lindbergh. He's gonna fly right over our house." Staring at the sky, Lee watched intensely as this world hero flew over their farm in his sleek, silver plane. It was an event Lee would never forget.

Another day Lee would not forget was the day the banker drove into the farmyard with his shiny, black car. "I'm look-ing for James Porter," the man said to the boys in a deep voice. Lee pointed to the house and replied, "My dad's in-side." Dressed in a dark suit and bow tie, the banker walked hastily up to the front porch and knocked on the door. Dad opened it and invited him in.

Lee, Raymond and John had followed the man up to the porch. "Now you kids go play," Mother ordered. "Your dad and I will talk to this man from the bank." The boys turned around and walked towards the barn. It seemed like a long time before the banker came out of the house. When he did, he left in the same abrupt manner in which he came.

A little while later, Dad came out of the house. He had a solemn look on his face. "Boys, it looks as though we will have to move. I'm going to be selling some livestock as we won't be able to stay on this land." When the boys asked why, Dad just mumbled something about hard times. None of the boys knew what that meant, but they soon found out that for them, hard times would mean upheaval and sacrifice.

For the next two weeks, Dad made frequent trips to town with livestock or goods to sell. The boys helped by cleaning out the barn and sheds where vacant livestock lots soon began to appear. All the hogs were sold except for a few sows, but the dairy cows were spared to supply the family with milk. The other animals that remained were the horses used to pull the wagon and belongings of the family during their move.

Selling livestock was understandable, but having to sell the land was hard to accept. It did not seem right that a banker could take so many things. How did Dad get into this situation? Would he be able to earn back the things he lost? Those were questions the boys had, but there was no way of changing the past. So they did as they were told.

Mother started packing dishes and clothes. She did not say much as she cleared the shelves. She was busy with cooking, washing and cleaning along with watching the children. Warren was a toddler and Jeanne was a baby starting to crawl. Changing and washing diapers by hand was time-consuming. Five-year-old Mary Jane tried to play with her younger siblings while Mother was busy. They could only be entertained for so long, however.

Sometimes Mother sang a lullaby or hummed a song to rock the youngest children to sleep. As she moved back and forth, she wondered how it happened that they were forced to leave this farm. Mother did not fully understand the banker's demands, but she knew they were behind on their payments for debts owed.

Being delinquent on payments was something Mother was not accustomed to. Having been married previously to a financially solvent man, money had not been a worry. In fact, a money problem was the last thing Mother could think of when her first husband, Frank, took his own life. Why would a successful farmer, happily married with two small boys, do such a thing? It was a mystery no one could answer. Each time Mother thought about it, she ended up dismissing her thoughts for this reason. Some of life's questions could never be answered on earth.

As Mother rocked some more with baby Jeanne in her arms, she thought again about the issue with money. After Frank died, she and her two sons (Lee and Ardell) inherited a significant amount of money totaling twenty-eight thousand dollars from her husband's estate and his family. The inheritance was kept in a bank in Solon, but unfortunately the money was handled in a negligent manner by its bankers. Mother later discovered that as a result, the balance remaining was only fourteen percent of this total amount or three thousand nine hundred and twenty dollars to be divided between the two boys. In addition, they also inherited twenty-five hundred dollars each from their grandmother which was protected. Neither boy, however, could receive his inheritance until the age of twenty-five.

Mother pondered over the thought of once having had that money and how it could have helped to pay the debts they had incurred. But what was done could not be changed. These were tough financial times and she and Dad would have to work diligently to manage their growing family.

Conesville House circa 1925

Lee, John and Raymond at Conesville house circa 1928

On a cold, damp morning early in March 1928, Dad started hitching up the team of horses to the wagon. Mother had packed her dishes and personal items with care to load into the wagon. Holding baby Jeanne, she helped the boys and Mary Jane climb in. With the livestock following, the team of horses pulled the load and slowly, the family made a seven mile journey to a farm located south of Nichols, Iowa.

Dad was able to rent this one hundred and sixty acre farm from a man named Smith. The Smith farm had a house in good condition with several outbuildings. The barn was big with ample room for the cows and horses.

Dad raised hogs in the fenced-in pastures and this meant there was meat for the growing family. Mother knew how to can the meat by salting and frying it down. She made sausage and liverwurst, too, cold-packed and covered with lard in sealed crock jars. This required grinding the meat and one time she bruised her right hand in the process. Her hand became swollen in the palm as if a boil had formed. Although it was awkward and painful, Mother still managed to do her daily work and her hand healed in time.

In November 1928, native Iowan, Herbert Hoover, was elected to serve as president of the United States. Unfortunately, the prosperity which the nation had reveled in during the 1920s was coming to an end due to a disruption in the world economy. In October 1929, the stock market crashed and in the months that followed, the value of stocks sharply declined, investors lost confidence, businesses and factories began to close, farm prices dwindled to record lows and ultimately, banks failed. This led to the start of the Great Depression, a period of financial difficulty for many.

Economic challenges during the Great Depression may have affected those in town more than people living on farms as food was plentiful from gardens and fields. The Smith farm was diversified and provided the family with a variety of food and produce to sell. This helped the family endure the financial strain largely associated with the Great Depression. Mother planted big gardens and preserved vegetables and fruits as soon as they ripened. Dad raised melons and sweet potatoes on the sandy ground. How Mother was able to fulfill her duties of gardening, cooking and washing clothes by hand was astonishing when she had a son, stepson, six young children, ages one to ten years, and was expecting another child. She had to be exhausted at the end of each day, yet she never complained.

The country school, called Lacy School, was two miles away from the farm. The Porter children who attended school would walk to it each day. In the winter when there was snow on the ground, Ardie would drive a sleigh, pulled by a horse, on which the children rode. Mother worried about them getting frostbite on their hands and feet.

Walking to and from school gave the children an opportunity to socialize with kids in their neighborhood. The children were generally well-behaved, but occasionally they would engage in a bit of mischief. There was never any fighting but rather, fun horseplay like throwing sand or teasing one another. One day, an older girl who attended high school in Nichols, walked up behind them and witnessed their mischievous behavior. She told their country school teacher, Miss Crow, they had been fighting. Miss Crow believed her and the next morning the boys were met by their teacher at school. She had cut switches from the bushes and proceeded to give Raymond, Lee and another boy a whipping.

John hung back and saw Miss Crow whipping the boys on their backs and legs. He quickly ran home, cutting across the fields to run the shortest route. Once at home he shouted out, "Dad, you need to go to school because Miss Crow is whipping the boys." Dad took the horse and wagon and stopped at the other boy's house to inform his father of the situation. Together they went to Lacy School to confront this teacher.

Dad was on the school board at that time and they had a lengthy discussion with Miss Crow. She did not lose her job but was given a stern warning. There were no more discipline problems, regarding the way she punished students, after that.

The older boys helped out in the fields by hoeing the weeds and tending to the garden. One day, Lee, Raymond and John were playing up on the roof of the machine shed before going out to the garden. Just at that moment, their neighbor, Anna, peered out her window and saw them. Anna was an elderly woman who lived with her husband, Gabe, across the road from the Porters. It seemed as though she had nothing to do other than watch the boys and then report them if they were mischievous. "Mr. Porter," Anna said, "did you know those boys of yours were goofing around on the roof of the shed?" "No ma'am, but I'll make sure they stay off. Thank you." Dad did nothing more except to tell them to keep off roofs. The next incident, however, was different.

Hoeing around the melons and potatoes could be a boring job for three young boys. It did not take long before they started throwing a few weeds or dirt at each other and the inevitable messing around began. "Hey, you boys stop that right now," Anna hollered from across the road. "You had better get back to work or I'll tell your father." The youngest of the three, John, yelled back, "Shut up, you old bag." The boys snickered and went about their work.

Before the day ended, Anna came over and told Dad what had happened. Dad did not say anything right away, but later in the evening he took the three boys over to Anna's house to apologize. Lee and Raymond only had to say they were sorry. Dad told John, however, that he had to kiss her. John turned pale and could not do anything more than to say he was sorry. On the way home Dad asked John, "Why did you call her that? You didn't see handles on her did you?" John did not answer but he caught a glimpse of the other boys grinning.

In the spring when the weather warmed up, the snow would melt and turn into puddles of water. The boys had fun wading through them even if it meant their overalls got wet. One night before going to bed, Lee wrapped his wet overalls around the pipes that extended into his bedroom from the kitchen stove.

The next morning, Dad started a fire in the stove to warm the chilly, damp house. Apparently the damper was open because the fire burned quickly, causing the pipes to turn red from the heat all the way up to Lee's bedroom. There, Lee slept with his overalls wrapped around the stove pipes. Suddenly, they caught fire. Mother smelled smoke and came quickly into Lee's room. Seeing the fire, she pulled Lee from his bed and yelled for Dad to bring up some water. Dad brought up a dishpan full of water and threw it on the fire. It was enough to put it out. Startled and scared, Lee ran down the steps yelling, "My pants are burning." Thankfully, Mother was there at the right moment to rescue Lee from what could have been a major fire.

The boys helped out where they could, but Dad sometimes employed a worker to assist him. In the spring and fall especially, there was extra farm work to be done with planting and harvesting crops. One year, Dad hired a man who went by the name of Doc. Finding it hard to provide for his large family, Doc asked Dad if he had any extra potatoes he could spare. Dad gave him a burlap sack and told him to go to the bin in the cellar and pick out what he needed. Doc was surprised to discover that the potato bin was next to Mother's five-gallon, wooden keg of homemade wine. Doc liked his liquor and somehow found an empty fruit jar. "I'm running out of potatoes again, Jim," Doc would often say. "Well, help yourself. There's plenty in the cellar," Dad would reply unsuspectingly.

One day, Mother was in the cellar and discovered the wine keg was not as full as it should have been. "Jim, I know this keg was nearly full and now it's almost half gone." Dad and Mother soon realized what was happening. Dad told Doc the remaining potatoes were rotting so he would not be able to take any more. No more wine disappeared after that.

Occasionally, Mother would go to the town of Nichols with the horse and buggy. The horse's name was Bill. One time, Lee rode with Mother to town and on the way back they stopped at their neighbor's house, the Ryan's. This couple brewed their own beer. Mrs. Ryan brought up a bottle from the wine cellar after inviting Mother and Lee in. She gave both of them a glass of the beer which was the first time Lee drank any. It was a small glass and he thought it tasted good. Mother enjoyed her glass as well and fortunately Bill knew the way home.

When early thaws would occur in the springtime, it was common for water to flow over the road because it had nowhere to drain. This happened one morning when Dad was going to town, driving Bill hitched to the buggy. Bill pulled the buggy half-way through the water west of the Smith farm, but then stopped and balked at going any further. Dad got off the buggy and stepped into the cold water and sticky mud to try leading Bill through it. Bill would not budge. This resulted in Dad turning Bill and the buggy around and going home.

Once there, Dad told Mother what had happened and said he was disgusted with Bill. Mother had often used Bill to drive her to town and they had quite a special relationship. She told Dad that she could get Bill to cross the water on the road. Mother was right. She drove Bill with the buggy behind him and when they came to the water on the road, he did not falter. He crossed through the water without hesitation. Dad was even more upset with Bill after he heard this.

Once, while living on the Smith farm, Dad developed a boil on his back that was as big as an egg. He was sick in bed for weeks. He could only lie on one side or the other and needed help to be turned. Mother spent much time helping him up or dressing the abscess. She was exhausted with trying to maintain the household, cook, clean and care for Dad. Lee and Raymond helped where they could, but they were too young to do the heavy work on the farm.

Finally, Mother sent for her sister-in-law, Ada, to assist her. Ada and her husband, Elmer, lived in Solon. Ada was a big help to Mother while Dad was sick. Despite this, it was not until the doctor came and opened up the boil that it finally started to heal.

There were not medicines available to treat people, and many times the remedies were homemade or based on tradition. When one of the neighbors across the road became ill with a fever, Mother went over to see if she could help. Mother made her own wine and used wild grapes in her recipe. She took some of her wine to the sick man and instructed his wife to warm it up as hot as he could tolerate it. "Now, drink that wine as quickly as you can and then cover up well," Mother told him. The next morning his fever broke and he felt better after sweating through the bedding in the night. Soon, he was his normal self again.

Mother had given birth to a daughter, Helene, in May 1931. A colicky baby, Mother later said, "I never took my dress off for six weeks as I tended to the fussy baby." With a baby and six other young children to care for, her days were very busy. She had finally been able to obtain a gasoline-powered washing machine and that made the chore of washing clothes much more convenient. Still, there was always patching and mending to do, as well as children to care for and food to prepare. Mother focused on her family and somehow managed to get her basic work done.

Dad and Helene 1932

Later in 1931, Dad was told by Mr. Smith that the farm was being sold. Once again the family was forced to move. There were not many places available as Dad searched for a farm to rent close to Nichols. Finally, they settled on a sixty acre sand farm owned by Dickie Ford. The family referred to this farm as "Sand 60."

2

LIVING ON "SAND 60"

T HE CONDITION of the house on "Sand 60" was far
from desirable. It needed a new foundation and struc-
tural repair. For the family, living on "Sand 60" meant no
running water, no inside plumbing, no electricity, no radio
or phone and no car most of the time. Mother used an iron
range, with a water reservoir that was heated, to prepare
meals in the kitchen. During the summer months, the range
created too much heat so she cooked and baked in the
basement where an old iron range stood on the dirt floor.
Water from the pump in the barn had to be carried into the

house for cooking and cleaning. Baths were given in a wash tub in the basement next to the old iron range. It was one bath followed by another using the same water for everyone. Winters were terribly cold and summers were unbearably hot.

There were no fences on "Sand 60" so Dad was unable to raise hogs. This eliminated the source of meat supply for the family. They did have milk cows to supply milk and cream and chickens which provided eggs. Mother raised poultry from the size of baby chicks to fully grown chickens. She prepared pens and little houses for each setting hen and fed them cooked, cracked corn mixed with skim milk.

Growing melons and potatoes for sale provided the main source of income for the family. Dad rented small patches of sandy soil from different farmers to plant and grow melons wherever he could.

One time after tending to a patch of melons, Dad and Lee were coming home for dinner with the horse and wagon when they stopped at the house of a friend, Elmer Pike. Elmer was a bachelor who enjoyed making his own home-brew. He invited Dad and Lee in for a glass of beer. This was Lee's second taste of beer. This time, however, it had a greater effect since he drank it on an empty stomach. Lee was pale by the time he and Dad left Elmer's house, and he had to lie down in the back of the wagon for the remainder of the ride home. Lee stayed outside that after-noon so Mother would not notice his altered state of health.

The baby of the family, Jim, was born in December 1933. Mother continued with her daily work until it was time to have this baby. In fact, neither Jeanne nor Helene even knew she was expecting another child. The day after Jim was born the girls were told that their baby brother had arrived during the night. With surprised looks on their faces, the girls peaked into Mother's bedroom and were amazed to see baby Jim cuddled next to her. The country doctor, Doc English, had driven out to assist with the delivery. The birth of Jim completed the family with nine children and one stepson.

Mother suffered through a sickness shortly after Jim was born. In fact, she was too ill to care for him and the children. Aunt Ada came once again to help with the do-mestic chores of the household. Baby Jim was cared for by a neighbor until Mother recovered. Aunt Ada was good to the kids and they enjoyed having her care for them. After a few weeks, Mother improved and was able to resume her daily routine.

The "Sand 60" farm was closer to the schoolhouse, Lacy School. Still, Mother would worry about the kids freezing their fingers and toes when they walked to school in the cold winter months. The children wore four-buckle boots over their shoes to keep their feet warm and dry in the deep snow and mud. Mother would pack a lunch and send it with the kids in a one-gallon, empty sorghum tin. Filled with sandwiches made from homemade bread, butter and sorghum, and gingerbread cake, the lunches Mother sent were delicious. She would tell them, "Your lunch should stick to your ribs," and it did.

When school was in session, Mother had fewer children to watch over at home. Jeanne was only four years old when she started school. She kept sneaking off when the older kids left in the mornings. Finally the teacher said to Mother, "Just let her go. If she wants to come to school she can come and stay." There were no laws in place as to the age a child had to be in order to start school.

Having been built in the late 1920s, Lacy School was one of the more modern schools in the Nichols area. Rural schools were one-room schools composed of several classes, with pupils spanning a variety of ages, taught by one teacher. At Lacy School, the Porters made up one-third of the enrollment with five families in attendance. The teacher only had fifteen minutes to teach each class, so the children learned to be responsible by keeping themselves occupied and working independently. Class sizes were small with three to five students in each. Children would listen in on the other classes and learn from their lessons, too. Older students would help the younger ones with their assignments as well.

The teacher's job went beyond educating the pupils. Other duties included carrying the coal, removing the ashes, building a fire, making sure the water supply from the pump was adequate, shoveling snow, dusting and sweeping. Sometimes the teacher asked the older students to assist her with these chores. When Lee attended eighth grade at Lacy School, he was paid fifty cents to help the teacher with these duties. Early in the morning Lee would start a fire in the furnace to warm the building. "Fifty cents!" Lee exclaimed when paid by the teacher. "I have a job, I'm rich." Later, Warren had this same job and was also paid a small amount to keep the stove heated with wood and coal.

It was common for teachers to board with families during the week, going home to visit their own families on the weekends. Mother often boarded teachers to earn extra cash for groceries. The money received was five dollars a week. There was hardly room for another person in the Porter home, but any money received was valuable.

Lacy School East of Nichols, IA circa 1930
The old schoolhouse sits to the left.

Students of Lacy School 1930

Families of Lacy School at picnic in 1931

In 1934 Lee started attending high school in Nichols. He was not in favor of going. He felt conspicuous having only bib overalls to wear. Mother would always keep them clean, but they showed their wear with multiple layers of patches. At last he was persuaded to go, and in due time was finally given new jeans and a belt to wear to school.

While Lee was in high school, he participated in baseball. The school did not have buses so the older players drove cars to the towns of their opponents. One of their games was played at Conesville. On the way back to Nichols, some of the boys decided to race each other on the dusty, gravel road. One car passed the other and created so

29

much dust that the driver never saw the vehicle in front of him. The car ran into it and caused a collision. As a result, three players in the car were killed and three others were injured. Lee would have likely been with the team that day, but his grades were low and he was not allowed to play. That was the only game he missed.

Lee walked several miles to attend school in Nichols. Occasionally, someone would give him a ride once he was on the main road. During the cold winter months, Lee boarded with the postmaster and his wife. He was a block away from school and did not have to endure walking miles in the severe winter weather.

Winter months during the 1930s were extremely harsh. The old house on "Sand 60" was drafty and cold. A potbelly stove in the kitchen was the sole source of heat on the main level of the house. Sometimes the heat from it got so hot that it turned cherry red from the wood burning inside. Surprisingly, the house did not catch on fire. The family gathered around the stove trying to stay warm. In the mornings, the children would often bring their clothes downstairs to dress by the potbelly stove after Dad started the fire. When the kids came home from school they would pile their coats on a bed downstairs. At night, Warren would often gather up this pile of wool coats and take it with him to bed for extra insulation. Several siblings shared bedrooms and slept with each other to keep warm. Mother sewed together layers of old woolen blankets and denim to make heavy quilts tied off at the ends. The feather ticking in the beds made it cozy with the heavy blankets on top.

Shoveling the deep snow became an arduous chore when drifts piled up high in snowstorms. Dad and Lee would shovel a path by hand from the house to the barn, but the drifts would be higher than their heads. Still, they had to reach the barn to tend to the livestock and bring water to the house. They struggled to keep a path open before the wind would drift it shut again.

One winter day in 1936, a bad snowstorm developed and turned into a blizzard. The Lacy School teacher, Miss Mills, lived with her parents and brother about three miles south-east of school. Her mother and brother came to get her in a wagon pulled by a team of horses. Without warning, the snowstorm turned so fierce that they could go no further than Porter's. The teacher's brother unhooked the horses and led them home, leaving Miss Mills and her mother, Maude, behind. Mother, of course, took them in without hesitation as a few more to feed was not a problem.

Miss Mills slept on chairs while her mother, Maude, sat in a rocker through the night. Willy, Mother's stepson, stayed up to oversee the fire in the stove. Having had a battery-powered radio, the three of them listened to radio station *WSM* from Nashville, Tennessee while sitting in front of the warm stove. At that time one of the popular songs was, *Nobody's Darling But Mine*, by Jimmie Davis. Keeping track of how often it played, they heard it twenty-seven times that night from the Grand Ole Opry House.

The snowstorms and the weather which followed were severe that winter. Miss Mills and Maude actually ended up staying for several weeks. Dirt roads were poorly maintained and not easily cleared. It would take a warm or mild change of weather to melt the snow off the roads. People did not travel once heavy snow started accumulating. In fact, snow blew and drifted so high that it would freeze over the fences. In such adverse conditions, Dad and Lee would pull a sled to the four corners of the road in order to obtain staple goods. The grocer in town would deliver them to that point for rural dwellers. The winter of 1936 was brutally long and everyone was relieved when Miss Mills and her mother went home.

One event the family did look forward to in the winters was the annual holiday program at Lacy School. Besides providing education, rural schools served as social outlets for neighboring families. The most exciting program of the year was the Christmas program. Since financial limitations prevented the Porters from celebrating Christmas at home with gifts and decorations, the school program was considered their family's Christmas party. At one such event, a seventh grade girl was leaning over to smell a fresh baked pie when Raymond came up and pushed her nose in it. Mother was embarrassed but she laughed as well.

Lacy School bustled with energy and excitement as the children practiced their songs and lines for the 1936 program. The teacher strung a line and tied a sheet to it to serve as a curtain to be closed between performances. Parents and families streamed into the little schoolhouse with their baskets of sandwiches, fresh baked pies and cookies to be shared with one another after the program. The children were excited, but also nervous, to present their songs to this attentive crowd of people. It was a fun and joyful evening for everyone.

Students of Lacy School 1938
Front row, far left: Helene, Second row, far left: Jeanne, Jane in
center, Warren on far right, Back row: Raymond and John

Even though Christmas was not celebrated at home, one year Mother had a big surprise for the youngest girls, Helene and Jeanne. Helene was five years old and Jeanne was seven. It was Christmas Eve and the older children went ice skating on a small pond in the pasture. They used skates that clamped onto their shoes. Helene wanted to go, but Mother told her she was too young and needed to stay home. Seeing Helene's disappointment, Mother said she had a surprise and would show her once the dishes were done. After the table was cleared and the dishes washed and dried, Mother went to the porch and came back carrying two new dolls.

Helene was overwhelmed with joy and excitement to see the pretty, new dolls. She had never had a doll before. A rolled up towel or rag was the closest thing she and the girls had to play with. Since Helene could not go ice skating, she was fortunate to have first choice of the two dolls. She chose the pretty, Shirley Temple styled doll. She beamed with delight as she held the beautiful doll tightly in her arms. Jeanne was given the other one when she got back from skating. That was the only Christmas present the girls were given.

Even after Helene received it, she still continued to pretend with rolled up towels so that nothing would happen to the precious, Shirley Temple doll. She placed it on a shelf to be admired for quite some time.

Later, Helene asked Mother if she could make some clothes for it from scraps of material. Mother was busy, but one day she told Helene she would sew clothes for her beloved doll while the children were at school. Excited and anxious to see what clothes Mother was making, Helene had trouble concentrating at school. She decided she would tell the teacher that she was not feeling well and needed to go home. Once at home, she gave Mother the same explanation. Helene was certain that Mother knew the truth, even though she said nothing. Still, it was worth the risk of being caught to be standing next to Mother by the sewing machine, marveling at the new clothes she created for her doll.

During Christmas vacations, Dad and the boys would cut trees in the timber and haul the logs home with a horse and wagon. A neighbor, Ben Oostendorp, would help by cutting the logs into firewood using a saw attached to the front end of his Allis Chalmers tractor. By the time they were finished, the boys would have a pile big enough to fill a large shed.

Nights were long as the daylight was short. Dad would read to the children using kerosene lanterns to provide light. The older boys looked through the *Sears* or *Montgomery Ward* catalogues, admiring the pictures of guns and rifles for hunting game. Lee and John once saved up enough money to buy a Remington .22 caliber rifle which cost thirteen dollars. It was a thrill for them to own a brand new gun.

The family also read the county newspaper, the *Muscatine Journal,* which included the comics. One strip Mother particularly enjoyed was called *Boots and Her Buddies,* by Edgar E. Martin. Another paper the family received and read was *Capper's Farmer*, a weekly farming magazine with occasional fiction. Nothing was wasted. After they finished reading the catalogues, they never threw them away but instead used the pages in the outhouse. Toilet paper was too expensive to consider buying. The softer, yellow pages were the first ones to be used, almost a luxury in themselves.

The two younger girls, Jeanne and Helene, frequently had trouble with earaches in the winter. Antibiotics were not manufactured yet so remedies for treating sore throats and earaches were limited. The doctor in Nichols, Doc Moench, swabbed sore throats with iodine, but this was not a cure for the ailment. Mother gave the girls cloth diapers to wear over their heads to keep their ears warm when they had earaches. The warmth helped ease the pain. Dad had his own remedy of blowing cigar smoke in the sore ear to aid in the healing. This remedy was not effective. When one of the kids was recovering from an illness, it was common for Mother to say, "You look like the running gears of a katydid or the last rose of summer." Time was the greatest healer.

There were few toys to play with growing up on "Sand 60." Occasionally a jar lid was discarded and the children used a stick to push it for amusement. The first bicycle the family had was an old, used one with wooden rims and no tires. Raymond pushed it all over the yard even though he could not ride it.

Later, they were able to obtain a bicycle that worked properly. Shared by the entire family, someone got on as soon as another got off, but everyone took turns. One way Jeanne managed to get a turn ahead of Helene was by finishing up her chore of washing the dishes before Helene was finished drying. It would appear as though the two girls were keeping up with each other washing and drying, but then Jeanne would slosh around a large amount of silverware in the soapy dishpan and announce she was done. This would leave Helene to dry all the silverware, piece by piece, and put it away. Jeanne would then be out the door and on the bicycle long before Helene could finish drying all the utensils.

To help pass time on long days or evenings, the girls would draw pictures and color. One day to surprise Helene, Mother told Lee to buy a package of crayons along with her groceries when shopping in Nichols. When Mother gave the crayons to Helene, she marveled at the shiny colors with their tips fresh and pointed. Her old ones were broken and dull so it was a special treat to have a new package. Just so she could savor the newness of the crayons, she refrained from using them for quite some time.

When the family played together, there was very little squabbling or fighting. Mother would remind them, "If you can't say anything nice, don't say anything at all." Any time the boys started roughhousing Mother would say, "You get right outside if you're going to scuffle in here." The worst punishment given by Dad was when he told the boys they had to kiss each other to make up if they were caught fighting.

Willy Porter was Dad's son from his first marriage. An only child, his mother had passed away when he was twelve years old. Willy was much older than the other children and there was friction among them. One summer evening, Lee was washing dishes as they all took turns helping out. Willy came along and gave Lee a poke in the behind. Lee turned around and threw the dirty, soapy dishrag in his face and then ran out the back door with Willy close behind him.

Lee ran swiftly and when he came to a barbed wire fence, he made a leap and cleared it. This helped him stay ahead of Willy as he cut through a field with Willy chasing after him. Lee ran to the Zybarth house where three bachelor brothers lived. Their names were Ed, Pat and Whiskey Jim. The Zybarths saw him coming and let him in while locking the door on Willy. Knowing that Lee would pass through the neighbor's apple orchard in order to go home, Willy picked an assortment of apples to throw at him. Lee waited at Zybarth's until dark and then quickly ran home. He made it home safely and later told Mother and Dad what transpired. Dad said nothing, but Mother voiced her displeasure with Willy for what had happened.

Mother was very frugal with her money. She would often sell her eggs and butter to the merchant in town to trade for staple goods like sugar, coffee and flour. Many times the older boys would walk to Nichols, almost a three mile walk, with large burlap sacks to exchange the eggs and butter for groceries. It was common for the family to eat fried eggs, golden fried potatoes and fresh, baked bread as their main meal at night. Mother peeled pounds of potatoes every afternoon in preparation for supper.

It was rare that the family had meat to consume. One year, Dad purchased a hog for six dollars from a man who wanted to sell the animal at the Nichols stockyards. He wanted to obtain a license for his Model A Ford and needed cash from the sale. Dad made a deal with him and unloaded the hog which was butchered shortly after. However, this hog was an old boar and so the meat was tough and almost inedible.

Mother was conservative with materials that were available. Overalls were mended with patches on top of patches, and dresses for the girls were made from empty flour sacks. She never had a pattern to follow but would sew the dresses together on her sewing machine powered by a foot pedal. The girls wore dresses and long cotton socks in the winter and colder months. They could hardly wait for the first warm day of spring when they deemed it hot enough to pull off their long, itchy stockings. If Dad caught them without stockings, however, he demanded they go back upstairs to their rooms to put them on again. In the summer everyone went barefoot. The sandburs were painful if stepped on, but they simply pulled them out and kept walking.

When school started in the fall, Dad would buy the boys two pairs of bib overalls and two shirts. All the children were fitted with new shoes. Knowing that the shoes had to last the entire school year, Mother made sure there was adequate room in their size. There was a shoe store in Nichols and the children would purchase their shoes there late in the summer. Once at home with their new pairs of shoes, they frequently took them out of the box to smell the fresh scent of leather and admire the shine. To wear new shoes to school on the first day made the children feel proud.

Mother had the added chore of cutting the children's hair. She had a pair of hand-operated hair clippers. Sometimes the kids felt like she was pulling their hair out instead of cutting it off. Both girls and boys wore their hair short. Later, the girls were thrilled to grow longer strands of hair so they could pin it back with a ribbon or bow. It was a new style and something different.

Jeanne's hair was stubborn and hard to manage. After working with it and noting the difficulty, Mother took Jeanne to a beauty salon in Muscatine, Iowa to get a permanent wave. No one in the family had ever received a permanent wave in their hair. Jeanne was excited and did not know what to expect. Unfortunately, the results were not favorable for her. The curl of the permanent wave made Jeanne's hair frizzy and it stuck straight out. She looked in the mirror and was horrified. "It's a fuzz ball and I look like an idiot." She wanted Dad to shave it off in the barn as if he was shearing a sheep. Eventually her hair grew out of the frazzled state but she was embarrassed for several weeks.

3

WATERMELON DAYS

A MAJOR SOURCE of income for the Porters was the cash sale of watermelon and cantaloupe. Acres of melons were planted in the spring with a hoe. In the summertime, Dad would cultivate the weeds with a one row, horse-drawn cultivator and the boys would hoe between the hills of melons and sweet potatoes. They owned two horses for farm work, but they were not a matched team. They were old horses no one wanted. One was big and the other much smaller. Their farm wagon was put together with left-over parts. The front wheels were wide-rimmed and small in size. The back wheels were the opposite being three times bigger with narrow rims. The wagon sunk in the sand and was very hard for the horses to pull.

When the boys worked in the hot fields, they would take with them a one-gallon, stone jug wrapped in a burlap sack to keep their drinking water cool. The crops of melons and potatoes would be weeded and cared for throughout the summer until they were ripe and ready for sale in August. Many people would come from surrounding towns to buy the produce. Sometimes the melons were traded for a load of apples. The family had a cave in the ground, where the air was cool and dry, to store their vegetables and apples.

When school began each year in September, it was fun for the kids to come home in the afternoons and go out to the watermelon patch. Ripe melons could be broken by dropping them on the ground where they easily split open exposing their red, ripe, juicy flesh. The kids would sit down in the patch to eat the fruit, enjoying their afternoon treat.

Left to right: Lee, Jeanne, Jane, Jim, Warren, Helene, John, Raymond

Dad would be kept busy tending to the melons once they ripened. Picking and selling the melons was hard work. Yet, word traveled about the produce and there was a steady flow of customers. An interesting group of people that would visit each year was a mix of Gypsies. They typically came on a Sunday. A man would drive a car with women clothed in long, raggedy dresses. When Mother looked out the window and saw them pull in, she would holler out to the kids, "Get in the house, Gypsies are here!" The kids would scamper up to the house in fear of these strangers. They would not know who they were but would quickly adhere to Mother's warning.

Dad would meet the group when they walked up to the wagons to look over the fresh produce. He was aware of their schemes as one or two would try to distract him while another would attempt to steal cucumbers or melons. Dad wore bib overalls and he kept his billfold in the chest pocket snapped shut. One time a Gypsy came very close to Dad and touched the pocket where his billfold was. "What's in your pocket?" the Gypsy asked. Dad quickly pushed her away and told her to leave. Everyone was relieved when they drove out.

In the summer months, a grocery man would drive a route through the country to sell groceries from his truck. The truck was enclosed with shelves filled with food items.

This was always a special event for the children as they knew they would get a piece of candy or gum if they sat quietly on the porch. Mother would meet with the grocery man and then select the items she needed from the back of his truck. Frequently, Mother would trade her churned butter or maybe one or two chickens that would not lay eggs in exchange for staple items. Sitting quietly and very still on the wrap-around porch, the children would wait patiently for their candy. They were always appreciative of getting such a special treat.

Willy would insist that Mother buy him a can of Prince Albert tobacco when the grocery man visited. He was the only one who smoked in the family and rolled his own. Mother did not appreciate his smoking or his insistence on having the tobacco, but being kind-hearted, gave in to his wishes.

One day the landlord, Dickie Ford, stopped at the farm to chat with Dad. Dickie Ford had a keen sense of how the economy worked. He had surmised a national depression was coming months in advance and withdrew his funds from the bank before the crisis hit. This made him one of the more well-to-do men in the rural community because he had cash readily accessible, although it was more than likely hidden somewhere in his home. Pulling into the farmyard with his fancy, new car, he always had a story to share with Dad. This time, the boys decided to play a trick on Dickie. While Dickie was talking to Dad, the boys placed watermelon rinds up against the tires of the car. As Dickie proceeded to leave, he knew something was wrong because the car started to spin. Dickie stepped on the accelerator and it spun some more. He kept trying to move forward as the watermelon rinds were flying out behind the wheels. Finally, he made traction and the car spun its way out of the drive. The boys giggled and laughed while they watched from a distance as the entire scene unfolded.

When Raymond turned fourteen years old, a man named Frank Moreland talked Dad into buying a used Model T car from him for twenty-seven dollars and fifty cents. Dad had not driven a car since he sold his Chalmers, a two seated touring car with side curtains. He was not accustomed to driving a Model T so at first he declined Frank's offer. "Oh, I see you have a teenage boy there who could learn to drive it," Frank said as he gestured towards Raymond. It was no secret that Raymond loved cars, and the thought of having one to drive was very exciting. Finally, Dad consented and the boys then had a car to drive. At that time, three gallons of gas cost fifty-two cents. Dad would give the boys money for three gallons which was intended to last them a week while driving to school in Nichols. The only way to check the level of the gas tank was to place a stick in it to see how empty it was. If the car ran out of gas, they found themselves pushing it into town to fill it up.

When Jim was four years old, he was riding with Raymond in the Model T Ford. While driving in the circle of the farmyard, somehow Jim fell out and was run over by the Model T. Tire marks were seen across his shoulders. Mother saw this happen and ran out to the yard in fear. She was more scared than Jim as he only complained of a sore neck. Mother had him checked by Doc Moench the next day but no injuries were evident.

On occasion, Mother and Dad went to dances held on Friday nights at the Odd Fellows Lodge in Nichols. They attended these dances during the summer months. A small band played with a squeezebox being the main instrument. Mother would fix her hair with a metal curling iron that she heated by putting the end down in the chimney of the lamp. When the iron was hot she made waves on the sides of her hair. Once, when Helene was six or seven, she stood and watched Mother as she fixed her hair. "Do you have to go, Mama?" Helene asked in a worried voice. "Yes," Mother replied. "You'll be fine with the older kids. We won't be gone all night." Helene watched Mother and Dad drive out of the yard in the old Model T wishing they would not go and hoping they would be home soon. Since Mother seldom went anywhere, it felt strange to have her gone for an evening.

Mother and Dad would sometimes host dances in their home. Dancing in the largest room of the house, the front room, they would sprinkle corn meal on the floor for wax after putting the furniture out on the porch. Neighbors would come, bringing food to share for a potluck meal, while music was provided by The Gideon Brothers. This was a small band made up of three brothers who played the guitar, accordion and fiddle.

The Porters had a variety of neighbors. There were a few who were more peculiar than others. The son of Dickie Ford, Richard, lived with his wife, Alice, a short distance down the road. They had a daughter named Mary who went to school with the Porter children. Alice relied on Mother for advice as they were an awkward family and did not quite fit in. She was not even sure if she was pregnant with Mary when one day she stopped in to visit Mother. "Mrs. Porter," Alice asked, "do you think I'm going to have a B?" She pointed to her abdomen which was starting to protrude. "Yes," Mother said, "it looks like one is on the way."

When Mary started school, she was in the same grade as Jim. She was a homely child and did not trust anyone beyond family. Her mother, Alice, would always accompany her to school. On the first day, Mary walked up to the teacher and then to the students introducing herself. "I'm Mary Margaret Ford," she said slowly with her eyes gazed wide-open. There was a heat register in the upper level of Lacy School and Mary would stand on it to warm herself in the winter. Sometimes the boys in the lower level teased her by hooting and hollering as if they could see up through the register when they really could not. "Don't look," Mary bellowed out as she grabbed her skirt to pull it close to her.

Mary's father had served in World War I and was afflicted with a psychological impairment. Once on a winter day, the Porters saw Alice and Mary running across the field from their house to Porter's. Alice, with her long, raven black hair, looked frantic as she and Mary ran into the house. "Mrs. Porter," Alice exclaimed out of breath, "help us, please. We escaped from Richard. He was holding us in the house and was putting snow in the stove. We managed to get away but are afraid to go back." Mother let them stay for a while. It was common for her to put another plate on the table for drop in guests.

The men in the neighborhood knew Richard needed medical attention so they kept apprised of the situation. Several of the fathers in the community took turns guarding the schoolhouse in case Richard appeared. Finally, he was committed to a facility to care for him in one of the bigger cities. Alice and Mary remained in their home where they lived together for many years. They were both untrusting and suspicious of others so they lived a secluded, private life. However, they did stay in contact with Mother and the Porters.

Occasionally, Raymond had the privilege of driving Mother and Alice Ford to town to shop for groceries. Alice would always crank the Model T to get it started. She was very strong and Raymond would intentionally leave the ignition off while Alice cranked. Only when Alice was nearly exhausted and her face flushed from exertion would Raymond turn the ignition on. It was doubtful Mother knew what was happening, but Raymond often pulled this prank. Alice was fortunate she never broke her arm while cranking because as the tension became tighter, the lever could have easily kicked back and spun around at a great velocity.

Another set of neighbors that seemed to follow the Porters as they moved to "Sand 60" was Gabe and Anna. The boys were on guard when they encountered them, knowing the history among themselves and this elderly couple. One day, Gabe and Anna were driving by Porter's house with their old, spotted black and white horse hitched to a buggy. The roadside was filled with bushes and overgrowth. Raymond and John saw them coming up the road. They hurried to hide in the bushes with slingshots they had made. When the horse and buggy got close to where they were, the boys fired off a shot with a rock. The old horse made a jump and fell over dead. Apparently it had a heart attack. Raymond and John thought for sure they had killed that horse.

The boys ran to the house as fast as they could. "Gabe and Anna's horse died out on the road." The boys were scared and looked sheepish. Mother and Dad looked at each other but neither said anything. Everyone survived the ordeal, except the poor horse that was near death anyway, and the slingshot was hidden for a long time after.

When community news traveled through the neighborhood, it would always be the subject of interest to those living simple lives in a mundane world. So when the story circulated about a woman shooting her husband a few miles south of the Porters, the boys naturally became intrigued with curiosity and decided to investigate.

Lee, Raymond and John walked the distance to the vacant house where this incident was reported to have taken place. Upon their arrival, they noticed that a glass window beside the door had been broken. This created a hole just big enough for them to slip through and enter the old, run-down house. Once inside, they looked around and made some interesting discoveries. Lee found a pistol. "Hey, maybe this is the same gun she used to shoot her husband. Who knows?" Lee claimed it and stuffed it into his pocket. John spotted an empty syrup jar filled with glass marbles while Raymond discovered a can of pennies.

As the boys were walking through the empty house, they heard a noise which sounded like footsteps. They stopped to listen and then heard the noise again. Startled and scared, they quickly hurried towards the door to climb out the small hole in the glass. It seemed like more of a challenge to get through this time. "Quick! We gotta get out of here," Lee yelled. One by one the three boys escaped with their treasures and returned home safely.

Later, they confessed to Dad where they had been. They told him about the noises in the old house and were certain that someone was in there with them. Dad listened carefully but then smiled and said, "Oh, boys, that was just the sound of squirrels you heard up on the rooftop." With puzzled looks on their faces, the boys were not totally convinced, but their story helped make the news a little more interesting in the neighborhood.

In 1936 on the Fourth of July, the Porter kids went swimming in a small waterway called Wapsie Creek not far from their house. The creek was shallow but there was a pool of water in one section that was deep enough to dive in. John dived into the water near a tree that leaned over the bank. Under its roots was a hole that went into the bank. He stuck his hand in and it felt like something grabbed him. When he pulled his hand out, it was skinned. He called the others to swim over and they prodded around with sticks until they determined a big catfish was in the hole.

Raymond and Lee ran home to get a spear they had made for spearing carp during times of high water. Waking Mother and Dad from their afternoon nap, the boys told them, "There's a huge fish trapped in a hole of the creek bank. We're gonna try and catch it with the spear." With the use of the spear and a four-tined pitchfork, the boys poked around until the large catfish came out of the hole and swam into the shallow water. "He's a monster," John exclaimed. "We can't let him get away." John took the spear and struck the fish near the tail and held it down while the other boys ran a fishing pole through its gills and mouth. Together they were able to lift the big fish out of the water and up on the bank.

Smiling proudly at their prized catch, the boys were in disbelief that they were able to retrieve this huge fish from the creek. They hurried home with it to show Mother and Dad. They, too, were in awe of the large catfish. "How on earth did you manage to catch such a big fish?" Mother asked. The boys smiled as they shrugged their shoulders. Dad brought out the scale to weigh it. They hooked the fish to the scale and watched carefully as the scale's marker jiggled back and forth. "Forty-three pounds," Dad hollered out. "Wow, that's a big one." The boys cleaned it and the family enjoyed a big fish fry for supper that night.

Lee, John and Raymond with big catfish caught in Wapsie Creek 1936

As mentioned, Mother was always generous when it came to putting another plate on the table for drop in visitors. There was a family, the Stevensons, who lived half a mile south of the Porters and their children visited frequently. Their large-sized family was also strained financially. Mother never turned anyone away and would offer the Stevenson children bread and butter to eat. Later in time, one of the Stevenson children told Warren, "The reason why we hung out at your place so much was because we knew we'd get something to eat."

Surprisingly, even hobos knew of the Porter's kind generosity. It was not uncommon for a hobo to stray into the farmyard asking Dad if he could spend the night in the barn. Dad consented and Mother sent out a sandwich for the hobo to eat. Sometimes the traveler had with him a fiddle to play. In one instance, a hobo began to play his fiddle when Dad told him that his daughter, Jeanne, could tap dance. She really did not know how to tap dance, but Jeanne made an attempt as the hobo played a song.

Jeanne was known for being ornery. One time Mother baked a cake and frosted it on all sides. She left it sitting on the counter in the kitchen. Jeanne happened to come in when no one was there. Tempted by the delicious-looking cake, she quickly made the decision to scoop up the frosting with both hands. With her fingers and hands full of sticky frosting, she ran out of the kitchen to hide and eat the sugary glaze. Mother later came in and was shocked when she saw the cake stripped of its frosting. After she discovered it was Jeanne who did this bold act, she sternly voiced her displeasure at what she had done.

The 1930s were distressing years to endure. Not only did the Great Depression make life challenging financially, the extreme weather patterns made it strenuous as well. Summers were unbearably hot. The summer of 1936 was extremely hot with temperatures soaring past one-hundred degrees day after day. The house never cooled off from one day to the next. Mother would still have to cook on the wood-burning stove in such heat. Often times the family slept outdoors at night to obtain relief from the hot, sticky air. The entire countryside was in a drought that summer.

The windows had no screens but were opened wide, as were the doors, to allow a breeze to flow through. The problem with that, however, was that flies also came into the house. Lee helped Mother shoo the flies out with dish towels, waving the towels to chase them out.

As the sun rose in the sky, the temperature inside the house increased as well. Butter in a dish melted into a puddle with no means to refrigerate it. After Mother churned the butter, the boys placed it in a bucket and lowered it into the well by the windmill to keep it cool. The family had no fans or ice. Milk for breakfast was placed in a tub of water, changed several times during the day to keep it cold. It was uncomfortable being outside in the hot sun, especially when the wind blew sand from the barren ground, stinging their eyes with grit and dirt.

Late in summertime, the boys would take a week to ten days to go camping and fishing on the Cedar River. It was enjoyable to relax by the water. Other recreation the boys would engage in was swimming in Wapsie Creek on warm evenings. It was another way to cool off from the hot summer heat.

As the 1930s came to a close, Dad's health began to decline. He developed a violent cough in the winter of 1939 and was growing weaker as the days passed by. If a doctor was needed, the boys had to walk to the neighbor's house to call because Porters had no phone. Mother kept on with fulfilling the requirements of her busy work day in the house, but she realized that her husband's health was not improving as he was in bed most of the winter.

4

OUR DAILY BREAD

T HE START of the new decade in 1940 marked the end of the Great Depression in America. Productivity, employment and consumerism were on the rise under the leadership of President Franklin D. Roosevelt. Several programs had been developed by the government to create jobs and offer new opportunities to spur economic growth. As a result of the aggressive invasions precipitated by Germany and Italy throughout Europe, the United States was beginning to produce and supply military equipment to England, France and its allies. This industry would have an enormous impact on the economy by creating jobs and helping to increase consumer spending, two major reasons the United States was able to move out of the Great Depression.

Life for the Porter family, however, proceeded in much the same way. Money was scarce and Dad's health was steadily deteriorating. Starting a new year in January meant three long months of cold, snowy weather lay ahead.

The old farm house was drafty and the aged wooden floors were cold. Early in the mornings, Mother would rise in the darkness to start a fire in the potbelly stove and iron range. Sticks, corn cobs and small pieces of wood were needed to start the fires. Mother's next duty would be to start her day of baking and cooking.

Every morning Mother would bake three loaves of bread and a large pan of biscuits. She would have already mixed the dough the evening before. Mother used a big stone bowl in which she prepared the dough from flour, eggs, milk and yeast. She would mix the dough by hand with a spoon and then set it aside to rise overnight, having completed her last chore before going to bed.

In the morning, the dough would be puffy and ready to be punched down. She kneaded it with her hands until it was ready to be shaped into three loaves and multiple biscuits. Once again, she would set the heavy, black iron pans of dough aside to let them rise. Mother never had cupboards or many utensils to work with. She kept what dishes and spoons she had on a table next to the range.

Later in the morning when the dough had risen again, she would use a feather brush to spread a little lard on the top of the dough. This helped to soften the crust. Once the range was heated, she would put the pans of bread into the oven to bake. Yet, she could not venture too far from the oven since the heat of the fire had to be monitored. If the heat became too hot, the bread had to be pulled out to avoid burning. There were no set temperatures or timers on the range. Years of practice made Mother an experienced baker and cook. As the bread baked, the aroma would permeate throughout the house, setting off a comforting feeling of Mother's love. Everyone looked forward to the meals they had with warm, fresh bread and the butter Mother churned. A little bit of molasses on top made it even better. It tasted so good.

Soon after, the boys would rise to start their chores outside. Mother would begin to boil water on the range to cook a big pot of oatmeal. Once the cow was milked, the milk would cool some and then the fresh cream was skimmed off and saved for Mother to later churn butter. After the boys finished feeding the horses and cow and gathered eggs the chickens had laid, they would come inside from the bitter cold to warm up by the potbelly stove. The cooked oatmeal was hot and always tasted good with the fresh milk.

A few minutes later, the girls would awaken and dress for school. Once everyone had eaten, it would be time to slip on the four-buckle boots over their long, cotton socks. It was a cold and cumbersome walk through the field to get to Lacy School. With mittens on their hands and hats on their heads, the boys and girls would start walking to school, facing the cold elements. Soon the sun's rays would start to shine and its light would glisten on the sparkling snow. The cold northwest wind would cut through the children as they made their way towards Lacy School. By the time they arrived, their cheeks would be chapped and their noses red from the cold winter air.

Whenever school was dismissed, the children made their way back across the field to the farmhouse where the sweet aroma of fresh, baked bread greeted them as they opened the door. The boys would hurry with their evening chores which included milking the cow, feeding the horses and gathering the eggs. Water from a pump in the barn two hundred feet away would have to be brought in as there was no water pump in the house. This was very inconvenient for Mother when she needed water to wash, cook and clean.

After the chores were finished, the family would sit at the table on a long, wooden bench and a mix of unmatched chairs to eat supper. Mother would prepare a delicious meal of fried eggs, golden fried potatoes heaped up in the black iron skillet, green beans she had preserved from her summer garden and of course, fresh, baked bread. It was the same supper the family ate each night, but no one complained. The food tasted so good and everyone was satisfied.

On Sundays, Mother would fry a small hamburger patty for each person, served with mashed potatoes and gravy and coleslaw. Sometimes she made a soft pie, like custard or sweet potato pie for dessert. Also on Sundays, a treat for the family would be to fix popcorn or taffy in a heavy iron skillet on the range. It was fun for the kids to pull the taffy.

It was a Sunday in February 1940, while the family was eating their dinner, when the city attorney drove into their yard. "That can't be good news," Mother said as she saw him get out of his car. Mother was correct.

Mother's oldest son, Ardie, from her first marriage, had left home after growing tired of Willy's bullying. He was the first of Mother's children to leave. After a few years, he met Jessie and they married and later had a son named Larry. The city attorney had come to tell Mother that for whatever reason, Ardie had taken his own life early that morning. Shocked and grief-stricken, Mother instantly thought back to when her first husband, Frank, had taken his own life

65

and left her with two small boys, Ardie and Lee. Again, it was incomprehensible why someone would do this, but some of life's questions would remain a mystery.

Mother was a strong person and never complained. She may have been sad and in mourning over Ardie's untimely death, but she did not reveal her emotions. She quietly continued to do her work in the house, staying focused and committed. Her mind was also preoccupied with the declining health of Dad as he grew weaker each day. Fortunately, Mother could confide in Miss Fedderlin, the teacher from Lacy School, who boarded with the Porters during the week. It was never a problem for Mother to put an extra plate on the table, and earning five dollars a week for boarding a teacher was an easy source of money. Mother could at least discuss with Miss Fedderlin the worries she had when Dad was sick.

When Dad could no longer get out of bed due to his weak heart, Mother asked the girls to take turns staying home from school to sit with him. Neither Jeanne nor Helene liked sitting with Dad. It was frightening for them to hear him groan in his weakness. He continued to be bedridden for weeks, unable to leave his bedroom upstairs. Along with her household duties, Mother tended to her husband and remained devoted even with the unwelcome realization that he would not recover.

On a spring day in April of 1940, with the older boys and Mother at his side, Dad passed away at the age of sixty-six. While the younger children were at school, word was later sent to their teacher about Dad's passing. At the end of the school day, Miss Fedderlin told Helene, Jeanne and Jim to wait with her. She told them she was going to take them to Nichols to buy Mother some groceries. Not being aware of Dad's passing, they did not know what to make of this unusual arrangement. Being typical children, they playfully scurried into her car, almost bursting with anticipation.

Of course, once they arrived at home the children heard the sad news. Miss Fedderlin helped Mother with preparation of food and making arrangements for Dad's funeral. It brought comfort to the family when neighbors and friends stopped by with food and offered their condolences. Some food, like bananas and homemade cakes, were special treats for them. This was exciting for the children as there was a variety of food, some of which they had never tasted before.

Throughout this period of grief and sorrow, Mother never wavered. Her spirit was strong and she continued to handle this grim situation in a calm and steady manner. She must have had so many worries on her mind, yet she did not appear to be distressed. Deep inside she was committed and resolved to keep her family together. Through her faith and the grace of God, they would remain together as one family.

Dad's funeral took place at the Methodist Church in Nichols. It was a cold, damp April day. Some of the children were given clothes to borrow, even though they did not fit properly. Helene wore a heavy coat that was oversized. She felt embarrassed by the way it hung on her and almost dragged on the ground. The family filled the front pew at the service and sat quietly while the minister spoke words of comfort from the pulpit. The congregation sang some of Mother's favorite hymns she had selected, such as *The Old Rugged Cross*. After the service, the family filed out of the church behind the casket and Dad was then laid to rest in the Conesville cemetery.

Some friends and family went back to the farmhouse to be with Mother and her family, like Aunt Clarey and Uncle Louis from Solon. Mother did not allow any music or radio to be played during this time of mourning. Eventually friends and neighbors left, and Mother, at the age of forty-six, was faced with the realization that she would be raising this large family on her own. Fortunately, Dad had a small life insurance policy which Mother used to pay for his funeral expenses. This also taught her the value of having life insurance and she later took out small policies on the children.

The older boys were responsible about doing their chores and helping with the farm work. They knew that melons and potatoes would need to be planted in the coming month. Strawberries also needed to be tended to as they had a large patch planted in the sandy field. The melons and potatoes were planted with a hoe and later cultivated with a one row, horse-drawn cultivator. Weeds would need to be hoed in between the plants during the summer.

With very little grass available, it was a challenge to find enough food for the cows to eat. Instead of hay, the boys would go to the swampy marsh of Wapsie Creek and cut slough grass to feed to the cows. Often the boys would herd them along the road to let the cows eat grass in the ditches. One day, John and Warren were given the responsibility of herding the cows. It was boring waiting with them so they decided to take a quick swim in Wapsie Creek while they grazed. After the boys had cooled off in the water, they came back to the spot where they had left the cows only to find them gone. After searching the neighbor's fields and ditches, the boys soon employed the help of other family members to join them. It was later discovered that they had grazed the entire way to the town of Nichols, three miles west of Porters. John was so upset with those cows for wandering off. Mother was displeased, too, and gave the boys a stern talk about leaving them unattended.

Mother kept busy with her daily routine of cooking and baking. Every morning she started a fire in the oven range before working with the dough that had risen overnight. Every day she baked three loaves of bread and a pan of biscuits. Not a day went by that there was not bread on the table.

Mother never learned to drive any car other than a Model T Ford. She frequently mentioned a new Model T she had purchased in 1913 when she was nineteen years old. (She had worked in a restaurant at the time and the cost of the car was three hundred dollars.) Having to rely on others for transportation, occasionally Mother rode into Muscatine with Dickie Ford to buy items of necessity. Helene did not like to see Mother leave. She felt insecure when Mother was gone for these short shopping trips. Mother never felt safe riding with Dickie Ford in his Model A car because he was known to be a reckless driver. In one incident in Muscatine, Dickie was driving up a steep hill on Green Street. The car struggled to make it up the hill and suddenly the engine died. Fearing for her life, Mother quickly opened her car door and scrambled out before it started to roll backwards down the hill. She always made it home, though, safe and unharmed. Sometimes she brought

Helene and Jeanne a surprise from the Woolworth dime store in Muscatine. For fifteen cents, Mother would buy them a bracelet or necklace to wear. The girls were elated.

The boys continued to hunt rabbits, squirrels and ducks when time permitted. Lee, John and Warren also trapped mink, muskrat and fox. Once they trapped a grey fox. The prices for pelts ranged from three to five dollars for red foxes, ten to twenty dollars for mink, three dollars for a big skunk, and a dollar and a half to two dollars for muskrat. Trapping provided spending money and the boys enjoyed it. One time John and Warren trapped three skunks. It was an ordeal working with the smelly varmints. Their clothes wreaked and Mother made the boys take them off and bathe. For the next two days at school, they carried an odor with them that penetrated throughout the building.

When duck season was at its optimum, the boys would bring home burlap sacks full of ducks that they had shot. The birds provided extra meat for the family. In the fall of 1940, an early blizzard in Wisconsin suddenly caused ducks to fly southward to avoid the abrupt change in weather. As they flew south into Iowa, the sky turned almost black with hundreds of ducks in the air. Warren and Lee took advantage of this opportunity by shooting as many as nineteen ducks that day.

Lee and John with a grey fox

Life for the Porters in 1940 continued in the same way it had when Dad was alive. The main cash crops were melons, strawberries and sweet potatoes. Mother managed the money from the sale of this produce wisely and efficiently, even though she did not have a substantial income to work with. Everyone in the family contributed to helping with the produce and worked harmoniously to make it profitable.

1940: Jim, Larry, Warren, Jeanne, Helene and Jane sitting on bushels of sweet potatoes

Mother thought about the inheritance Lee had received from his father and his grandmother, and the amount of money which was lost through the bankers' negligence years ago. She was angry that so much of the money had slipped away, but was determined to see if Lee could obtain this inheritance at an early age. Mother had Dickie Ford drive her into Muscatine to meet with an attorney to discuss this situation and the hardship she faced. She explained to the attorney that Lee would be turning twenty-one years old in February of 1941. Instead of waiting until the specified age of twenty-five to receive his inheritance, could he possibly receive it at age twenty-one?

The attorney understood Mother's plight and agreed to help her. He was able to persuade the county judge to release Lee's inheritance at the age of twenty-one. This was a huge victory for Mother as it meant that Lee would be receiving twenty-five hundred dollars left to him by his grandmother along with a smaller inheritance of nineteen hundred and sixty dollars bequeathed from his birth father.

Late in 1940, Lee told Mother he knew of a farm with one hundred and sixty acres that was for sale south of Nichols. Knowing that he would be receiving his inheritance in February, Lee made a deal with the owner. The owner accepted the terms to sell the farm on contract to Lee for thirteen thousand six hundred dollars (eighty-five dollars an acre) and the inheritance money was used as a down-payment. With the help of a bank in Wilton, Iowa, Lee was ready to start operating this farm in 1941. A new opportunity for making a decent living was in sight for the family.

Mother was elated to know that they would be moving to this one hundred and sixty acre farm that they would soon be the owners of. The house was in much better condition, structurally, than the old farmhouse they had been living in on "Sand 60." Lee did not have very much equipment to work with, but with Mother's guidance and encouragement, he forged ahead with the purchase of this farm.

John was especially excited about the upcoming move to the new farm. Helene overheard John and Lee talking about the new opportunity prior to moving. "It's really going to be great, Lee, to have our own farm to live on and to call it our own. I can't wait to move there."

5

A NEW FARM

L EE RECEIVED his inheritance shortly after his twen-
ty-first birthday in late February of 1941. The family
quickly began preparing for their move to the new farm
which was two and a half miles southwest of where they
were living. March 1st was the common date for taking
possession of land when ownership changed. Moving with
horse and wagon, the family was anxious to get settled into
their new home.

In addition to their own family, Mother's daughter-in-
law, Jessie, was also staying with them along with Jessie's

young son, Larry. Following the death of Mother's oldest son, Ardie, in early 1940, Mother asked Jessie and Larry to join them. Jessie was good company for Mother and the younger girls loved to play with baby Larry. Later in the year, with Mother's encouragement, Jessie decided to attend school at the Iowa State Teacher's College in Cedar Falls, Iowa to obtain her teaching certificate. Jessie attended classes during the week and came home on weekends while Larry stayed with the family. Eventually Jessie received her teaching certificate and was able to secure a teaching job at a country school nearby.

The house on the new farm contained a summer kitchen where Mother did her cooking, baking and washing. No longer did she have to go up and down stairs to use the range or washing machine. There was also a pump on the back porch which made it much more convenient when needing water in the house.

The wringer washer was placed in the summer kitchen and clothes lines were strung. Mother would hang the clean, wet clothes on the lines year round to dry in the fresh air. There was no electricity or plumbing in the house, but these features would soon be added.

The outbuildings on the farm were in good condition, too. There was a large-sized barn, machine shed, hog house and corncrib. The family made wise use of the land and buildings, diversifying their farming operation. In addition to growing corn and oats, the family also had forty acres of hay which they rotated with the acres of corn. Strawberries, melons and potatoes were raised and sold retail. Finally, the buildings gave them an opportunity to raise livestock which provided the family with another source of income as well as fresh meat to consume. Mother continued to plant a big garden full of green beans, tomatoes, cabbage and other vegetables she preserved for winter.

Lee was limited in the amount of equipment he had when he began to operate this farm. The bank loan helped him get started, but he relied on the goodwill of neighbors to borrow their machinery in order to plant and harvest crops. This meant that the boys did their field work in the evenings when the neighboring farmers were not using their equipment. Largely as a result of World War II, farming was becoming more profitable as prices of grain and produce were increasing.

It was springtime and the crops were being planted in the ground. After the oats, corn and alfalfa were planted, the strawberry plants were set out in a big patch, the size of one acre. Next the melons and potatoes, both Irish and sweet potatoes, were planted. Mother was busy working in her garden as well as tending to her other daily duties.

Every day Mother would rise in the mornings to knead the dough which filled a large, iron pan with three loaves and another pan with biscuits. She also had baskets of washing to do which included bib overalls and dresses. At least she could conveniently do her washing and cooking in the summer kitchen which was close to the main kitchen.

In the late afternoons, Mother would start the evening meal by peeling a dishpan full of potatoes. She would sit at the kitchen table with the potatoes in front of her and carefully peel the skin from each one. She would then slice them and place a heaping pile of potatoes in a big, black skillet. Adding a small amount of lard, Mother would cook the potatoes until they were golden brown. The standard evening meal of golden fried potatoes, fried eggs, green beans or tomatoes and fresh, baked bread was delicious.

All of the children took turns helping do the dishes. After the table was cleared, Mother would wipe off the oil cloth table cover. She always leaned forward to reach the outer edges of the table by supporting herself with her left hand, the first and little fingers extended forward with the middle two curled underneath. Occasionally, Mother would use a small amount of oil to polish the table cover. It looked like new when she was done with a slick and shiny finish.

The younger children no longer attended Lacy School since they now lived too far away. Their new country school was called Pike School and it was a short distance to the south of their house. The older children attended high school in Nichols. Raymond graduated in the spring of 1941. John was a junior, then, and Jane was a freshman.

Lee, John and Warren often went hunting on the weekends for squirrel, ducks, geese and rabbits. Their dog, Jake, would accompany them. They would bring home burlap sacks full of ducks or fowl they shot. After cleaning the birds, they would clean their guns on Sunday evenings, spreading the parts out on the table to be cleaned and oiled.

One time when the boys were in the kitchen cleaning their guns, Willy took a glass straw and blew hard tapioca beads through it to shoot towards them. He got a few shots off when John, strong and athletic, reached over and grabbed Willy by his collar. He pushed him up against the wall and whispered through his teeth, "Don't ever do that again." Willy knew he was under matched with John so he sheepishly put the straw away.

Lee, Warren and John with Jake the dog

One of the popular songs at that time was *You Are My Sunshine*, recorded by Jimmie Davis. Mother loved this song and often sang the lyrics. Another song that Mother sang or hummed was, *When It's Springtime in the Rockies*, by Robert Sauer and Mary Hale Woolsey. Many afternoons you could hear Mother sing these songs while rocking Larry to sleep.

At last the family was enjoying ownership of their land and had a diversified farming operation in place. By the grace of God, Mother was given the wisdom to forge ahead with this opportunity and encouraged Lee to accept this challenge. Her fortitude and determination to keep the family together was unyielding, and she succeeded in many ways.

6

A CHANGE IN THE WIND

S UMMER was at its peak by July 1941. The corn crop was growing and the melon and potato plants were starting to blossom. The melon plants had grown vines and small melons were developing on each plant. The alfalfa had already produced one crop of hay and the oats were starting to turn color and ripen. Soon it would be time to shock and thrash the oats as the neighbors were getting their machinery ready to harvest the summer crop. The farm was in good condition and the family operation appeared to be working well.

Summer days were hot and humid in July. Mother would rise early in the morning to start her day. Before anyone else was awake, she had bread rising in the pans, and several lines full of clean, wet laundry hung to dry. It was wise to bake in the morning hours before the rising sun started to heat up the earth. Warm, humid air would fill the house creating a sticky feeling when anything was touched. Beads of perspiration would form on one's face when doing even the least amount of work. The heat and humidity made it unbearable when this weather pattern lasted for days.

Mother continued with her work inside and out of the house. She was busier than usual this week because the girls were out of town. Each summer they visited Mother's sister, Aunt Clarey, in Solon for a week to spend time with relatives. It was always a pleasure to go to Solon. Aunt Clarey baked delicious fruit-filled pastries called kolaches and other homemade goodies. It was fun to stay at her house and play with their cousins. The girls looked forward to their visit each time. This year they went to Solon during the first week of July.

After breakfast was served and the dishes washed, Mother would hurry out to the garden to pick string beans. The beans grew fast on the vine and they would need to be picked before getting too big in size. Mother would snap the beans from the vine and toss them into a bushel basket. She would fill many baskets heaping full.

Picking the beans was the first step in Mother's preparation to preserve them for winter. After she snapped off the ends, she would wash them in a dishpan and then proceed to cut them into small pieces. To preserve the beans, Mother would first place the raw vegetables in water-filled jars, sealing them tightly with metal lids. She would then put the jars in a large, copper kettle which held eight quarts of water. Setting the kettle on the range, Mother would heat the water until it came to a steady boil. The vegetables in the jars would cook in the boiling water for several hours. It was time-consuming to control the temperature and oversee this process known as cold-packing. It was also beneficial to work at this task early in the day before the house would become uncomfortable due to the sultry heat and humidity.

Mother preserved many jars of string beans that first week in July. She was pleased that her garden was producing a fine harvest of vegetables on the new farm. The tomatoes were developing nicely as well with their vines supporting several small tomatoes, still green and small in size. In a month the fruit would be fully grown, red and ripe to eat or preserve.

At the end of the week, Mother proudly admired the rows of preserved vegetables she had accumulated on her basement shelves. When winter arrived, there would be jars of beans and tomatoes readily accessible to make vegetable soup or to add to fried eggs for a nourishing meal.

It was not uncommon in the summer months for thunderstorms to develop with damaging winds in the plains of the Midwest. Iowa was no exception. Weather was not forecasted so people became accustomed to watching the skies for changes that would occur. Dad used to say, "It's lookin' a little squally in the west," when the sky became dark with clouds and looked threatening. It was during the first week of July, that summer, when the weather did change with unfavorable consequences.

Mother began the day like any other, mixing dough to prepare loaves of bread and washing clothes with the gasoline-powered washer. She knew it was going to be hot as the red sun started to peer above the horizon in the east. With no clouds in the sky, the earth would heat up quickly. Mother tried to complete her house work as soon as she could to avoid heating the oven in the hot afternoon.

The boys worked in the fields in the morning hoeing the melons and potatoes, but they also knew it would be unbearable to continue in the afternoon. After lunch was served, they told Mother they were going to fish at the river

86

to cool off. She agreed that it would be a good way to obtain relief from the stifling heat.

As the day progressed, the sky turned cloudy late in the afternoon. Grey clouds started to appear from nowhere in what had previously been a clear, blue sky. The boys were having good luck with the fish biting that day. Sometimes that happens before a storm as animals can sense a change coming. The boys had also been watching the sky and decided to pick up their gear and start walking home. The clouds were thickening and it was banking up in the west.

As the boys got closer to home, lightning strikes flashed throughout the sky. The wind started to increase, blowing dust and sand in sheets across the road and fields. Sand pelted their faces, making them feel like they were being cut by the sharp grains that were forcefully driven in the air. The boys started running and hurried to take shelter in the garage as rain started to fall. They waited anxiously next to the Model B Ford for one to two minutes and then decided to run quickly to the house as the storm intensified.

Warren, who was thirteen years old, started out running but then stopped half-way there, frightened by the fierce wind. He almost turned around to go back to the car in the garage. Fortunately, he decided to keep running and made it safely to the house. Just before he entered, he looked up to see the outhouse flying in the air along with other debris. Shaken by what he saw, he darted inside to take shelter.

The boys no more than got inside the house when they heard the roar of wind sounding like a train. Branches and pieces of wood started hitting the exterior. They heard creaking and the house shook. "Get in the basement, now!" Mother hollered. It was certain that a tornado was wreaking havoc on their property. Mother waited nervously with the boys in the basement as they all wondered what was happening to their farm outside. She paced the floor until the wind died down and the heavy rain from the storm stopped falling. When they came upstairs, they could not see out the windows because they were plastered with leaves and dirt.

Once they opened the door to take a look outside, their hearts sank with disbelief. At first it was hard to comprehend what had happened. Rubbish, boards, branches and tree limbs were scattered throughout the farmyard. Looking closer, however, they began to realize what devastation had taken place. The tornado had moved the barn off its foundation, destroyed the corncrib, knocked down the windmill, and flattened the garage. It was the same garage the boys had been standing in just minutes before. By the saving grace of God, they made the decision to take shelter in the house.

Oddly enough, the Model B Ford was left unscathed by the wrath of the tornado. Boards from the flattened garage laid in pieces all around the car, but the car itself remained upright with no significant damage. The windows had not even blown out. It was amazing to think it had not been destroyed. The fate of the car was not known at this time, but later the irony involving this vehicle would be revealed.

1932 Model B Ford escaped damage

Windmill destroyed in storm

Debris from corncrib scattered about

Mother was visibly shaken at the sight of downed trees and buildings destroyed. The scare of the storm and the damage it had caused was shocking to the family. The boys walked through the farmyard to survey the destruction. Thankfully, the house was spared, as was the chicken house and hog house. Boards were thrown and scattered into fields for miles. The majority of the debris landed in the neighbor's yard just east of Porter's farm. Branches were sheared off and trees torn apart. It was a sobering moment for Mother and the boys as they slowly began to clear the mess from that powerful storm. Neighbors came and helped with the clean-up as well. As property owners, the family had insurance on the buildings, and they were able to rebuild in the fall.

The effects of the storm were disheartening for the family after making such remarkable progress with their new farming operation. Still, they were resolved to continue and Mother, especially, was committed to move forward with rebuilding. No lives had been harmed in this storm and for that, Mother was grateful.

7

MOTHER'S STRENGTH

A S THAT FIRST WEEK of July came to a close, the skies cleared and the hot sunshine returned. It was Sunday, July 6th and Mother knew the girls were coming back that day from their stay in Solon. Aunt Clarey and Uncle Louis were bringing them home later in the afternoon. Lee and John had plans to play baseball in Nichols. They decided to take an afternoon nap before going.

The hot, sunny weather, however, made for optimal conditions to shock oats. One of the neighbors called to say that his oats were ready to be harvested and he needed some help. The common pay for hired help was thirty-five cents an hour. Rain was expected later that day so he was in a hurry to get his oats shocked. Lee and John said they could help and ended up skipping their ball game.

Shortly after two o'clock in the afternoon, Lee and John climbed into the Model B Ford with Lee driving and John riding in the passenger's seat. There was a small ridge or incline that was just north of Porter's driveway. When Lee pulled onto the road, a car was coming from the north at a speed of forty miles per hour and the two vehicles collided. The collision was so forceful it spun the cars around and left them side by side in the ditch. Both Lee and John were partially thrown out of their car.

Mother was inside dusting furniture when she happened to look out the living room window and saw the entire accident transpire before her eyes. Jim was playing outside in the front yard when he heard a loud crash and saw thick dust on the road. Mother ran out of the house screaming. Jim started to walk towards the road when she grabbed him by the arm and said, "No, don't go over there. You stay right here." Mother was shocked by what she had witnessed and called out for Raymond to come quickly.

A neighbor also saw the accident and called for help. Soon Raymond and several men were at the scene to do what they could. The people in the other car were injured but their lives were not threatened. Lee was badly hurt and the men helped extradite him from the vehicle as he was unconscious. Doc Moench came out to the scene and began to assist the accident victims. After assessing the situation, he walked up to the house to give Mother the grim news. He told her there was nothing he could do for John. He had died from the impact of the crash. Lee needed urgent care at the hospital for his serious injuries. Mother was numb after hearing this shocking news.

Meanwhile, Warren was playing baseball in Nichols at the school. Willy came and told him what had happened. Warren said they needed to get home as fast as they could. For some odd reason, Willy went the wrong way and started driving east. Warren shouted, "What are you doing driving this way? We live south of town, for Pete's sake." By the time they reached the accident site, Lee had been freed from the wreckage and was being transported to the hospital in Iowa City.

At the same time, Aunt Clarey and Uncle Louis were on their way home with the girls. It was common for Aunt Clarey to stop at Schaefer's grocery store in Nichols to buy a package of cookies to bring to Mother. Not knowing anything yet about the accident, Aunt Clarey told Helene and Jeanne to go into the store and pick some out. She gave them some money and the girls went in. While selecting the cookies, Helene overheard the grocery clerk talking on the phone, "Oh my goodness, that poor Mrs. Porter. How much more can that woman take?" The clerk, of course, did not know that Helene was Mother's daughter. Helene did not know what the conversation could have been about so she never mentioned it to Aunt Clarey when she got back into the car.

As Uncle Louis drove closer to the farm, the girls saw several cars parked along the road and in the driveway. They also noticed the corncrib was gone and other damage caused by the tornado. Upon entering the house, they discovered the tragedies that had happened in one week. Mother was sitting in the rocking chair, sobbing and crying. It was the first time the children could ever remember seeing Mother cry. For all the grief and misfortune she had endured, this was the first time they saw their resilient mother release her emotions in this way. The family stood in silence, not knowing what to say or do, while Mother's tears quietly flowed.

Aunt Clarey and Mother were very close and it was good she was there to support Mother. She and Uncle Louis stayed into the evening and then left with several loads of laundry that Aunt Clarey would wash and clean for the family. They came back later in the week for John's funeral.

Many of the neighbors stopped in with food and stayed to talk with Mother or offer their condolences.

Lee was being treated at the hospital in Iowa City. Not knowing how critical his injuries were at the time of the accident, it was days before Mother realized how severely injured he was. He suffered from a fractured pelvis, skull fracture and was in a concussion from Sunday through Wednesday. It would be weeks before Lee fully recovered.

John was a handsome-looking, seventeen-year-old boy with blonde hair. He was known for his athleticism and excelled in all sports at Nichols High School. He loved to hunt and fish as well. It was almost unthinkable how he survived severe damage from a tornado when the garage he was standing in days before was instantly destroyed. Within minutes after John left the building, it was gone. Yet, the tornado left the car unscathed. Ironically, this same car was the vehicle John was thrown from when it collided with another. The pain of this irony was almost unbearable. Mother had now buried two husbands and lost two sons in her lifetime. She was forty-seven years old when John was killed.

The funeral for John was held the following Tuesday afternoon at the Methodist Church in Nichols. The Porter family sat quietly in the front pew and tried to find solace in the minister's words. Hymns sung included, *The Old*

Rugged Cross and *Rock of Ages*, songs chosen by Mother which she found to be comforting. The church was filled with John's friends and classmates as he was very popular in school. Tears of sorrow flowed and sobbing was heard throughout the church. Following the funeral, John was laid to rest in the Conesville cemetery close to Dad's grave-site. Once again, Mother did not permit any music or radio to be played during this time of mourning.

Warren took John's loss especially hard as he and John were very close and spent much time together hunting, trapping and fishing. It took Warren nearly three years to accept what had happened and he often had dreams about John.

Mother had been given the foresight to purchase insurance policies on the children after Dad passed away. Fortunately she had this policy to cover funeral expenses for John when he was killed. She also used some of the money to purchase a dress and later, a new sofa and chair for the living room. The family never had furniture like this.

Lee spent the next eight weeks in a body cast. When he was released from the hospital, he was bed-ridden at home. Mother spent time caring for Lee as he recovered from his injuries. Even when he was able to stand up, he could not walk. He slowly and painfully began to take small steps. Raymond assumed the farming duties with support from the other children. By September, Lee was still too weak to lift a melon. He slowly regained his strength by the end of the year.

Mother had to deal with another worry after the accident, too. She received word from the city attorney that the other party involved in the accident was considering a legal suit against Lee for failure to yield. Mother was worried that they would sue and if they won, the farm the Porters had worked so hard to obtain could be lost. The attorney was a kind and thoughtful gentleman, and he realized Mother had experienced adversity and periods of hardship. He was able to persuade the other party to drop their charges and not go through with the lawsuit. What a relief for Mother.

Neighbors were considerate and helpful to the Porters when they came together to shock their oats as a community project. Women also came to cook a meal and serve lunch for the workers. It was a big day but the oats were harvested at the end of it, thanks to the goodwill of caring friends and neighbors.

Shocking oats at the Porters in July 1941

*Women helped with food preparation
when oats were shocked at Porters*

In the fall of 1941, the family felt a mix of emotions. Their first crop of corn yielded well, and the farm was profitable with melons, potatoes and grain producing a good harvest. The livestock had an ample amount of feed for the upcoming months and the barn was filled with hay and straw. The family was benefitting from their decision to purchase this farm as it was providing a decent income. The loss of John, however, remained a heartache for them to endure.

Mother's strength held the family together during this sorrowful period. It was the same strength that bonded the family together after Dad died. She never complained and never stopped working to provide food and basic necessities for the family. Her family came first and they knew they could look to her for support, even when times were trying.

As the year came to an end, the world was changing rapidly with World War II now coming closer to home. Japan, one of the Axis powers, was engaged in battle with Allied forces in the Pacific Ocean, which included its islands. On December 7, 1941 the entire family was in the field picking ear corn. Helene and Jim were the youngest so they took turns picking corn and driving the horse and wagon. The rest of the family picked corn by hand. One full load was picked in the morning and another in the afternoon. When they came inside for lunch that day, they turned on the radio and President Roosevelt was talking about the bombing of Pearl Harbor by Japan. It was now a certainty that the United States was directly involved in the war. How this would affect Mother and her family would unfold in the coming years.

8

WE ARE FAMILY

L EE GRADUALLY recovered from his accident and was able to resume his farming duties in the spring of 1942. Preparation was made to grow a variety of crops ranging from corn, oats, alfalfa, watermelon, muskmelon, sweet potatoes, Irish potatoes, strawberries and even tomatoes. Lee had planted three acres of tomatoes that year for H.J. Heinz Company in Muscatine. He hired a local trucker to haul three tons of tomatoes to the nearby town of West Liberty where they were to be delivered, but instead they were rejected. Unfortunately when the tomatoes ripened that summer, they had developed small brown spots and H.J. Heinz Company did not accept them. In addition, Lee had to hire helpers to pick the tomatoes in baskets. The tomato crop was not a profitable one that year.

The boys continued to borrow machinery from the neighbors to use when planting and harvesting their crops. During nights and on weekends the equipment was available so the boys operated the tractor for long hours, even through the night. The corn that was planted would later be harvested by hand in the fall. Using a neighbor's horse and wagon, the corn was picked, husked and then tossed into the wagon. The horse would patiently wait to pull the wagon ahead as the boys worked through the rows of corn stalks, husking the ears of bright yellow corn and throwing them into the wagon.

When the wagon was filled with corn, the horse would pull it to the corncrib where the corn was scooped eight feet high into the bin. One wagon load at a time, the corn went into the crib where it was stored as feed for the livestock. It often took a half day to fill the wagon with one load of corn.

Watermelon and muskmelon, also called cantaloupe, were sold from the farm. Customers came from miles away to buy the produce. The Porters sold retail and wholesale. A sale in August of 1942 for two hundred watermelons resulted in each melon selling for forty cents. Muskmelon sold for thirty cents each and one hundred and thirty-five of these melons were sold on a single day. Also in August of 1942, thirty-three bushels of muskmelon were sold for one dollar and twenty-five cents per bushel. Sales continued on a daily basis until the produce was gone.

Willy Porter, Mother's stepson, would frequently take a truckload of melons to be sold in bigger cities. Unfortunately, he would come home penniless with nothing to give Mother after spending or squandering the proceeds elsewhere. It was common for him to buy a box of chocolate-covered cherries and later eat them in front of the other kids. "Wouldn't you all like to sock your teeth into these?" he smirked as he gobbled up the candy. Jeanne and Warren once found a way to get even with Willy when they found his stash of chocolates. Willy had locked them in his cedar chest, but Jeanne and Warren pried the lid off with a screwdriver. Then emptying the box, they filled it instead with corncobs.

Mother was always busy with her garden in the summer months. She would annually set out new strawberry plants in the spring and planted rows of string beans, tomatoes and other vegetables during the same time period. When the strawberries ripened each summer, she hired people from Nichols to help her pick the luscious fruit. Mother paid them four cents a quart to help her pick strawberries.

If the weather conditions were optimal, the strawberry season would last three to four weeks. All of the kids helped pick the berries as they turned color and ripened each day. It was critical to pick them before they spoiled.

In the fall, sweet potatoes and Irish potatoes were dug from the ground to be harvested and sold. When the sweet potato crop was plentiful, the boys stored the vegetables in the Sweet Potato house. This was actually a small cave that had been created by digging out a large hole in a piece of land surrounded by trees. Small steps were constructed that descended to the dirt floor of this storage shelter. Inside, the air was cool and dry which made ideal conditions for storing the produce.

For a short while in the afternoons, Mother was able to rest and would tune in the radio to listen to *Ma Perkins,* a radio soap opera which aired from circa 1930 to 1960. The featured star was a widow who had a kind heart and offered to help those in need of advice. It was a fifteen minute show and was sponsored by Oxydol soap detergent. Listening to the radio and reading the *Muscatine Journal* were interests Mother made time for in her busy day.

One of the family's favorite radio programs was called, *Fibber McGee and Molly,* which aired from circa 1935 to 1959. The comedy radio show was famous for its episodes about "The Closet." Fibber's closet was very cluttered and an assortment of items would roll out whenever it was opened.

With the United States now involved in World War II, citizens were told they needed to conserve certain raw materials. One of the programs the government introduced was war rationing of consumer goods. Throughout 1942 to 1945, many goods such as sugar, coffee, gasoline, tires, shoes and cheese were rationed. Each family received coupons based on family size. The Porters were given several coupon books due to the large size of their family. They had few shortages of these goods in their house.

The boys and Mother were always interested in the updates of World War II. They listened intensely to radio addresses from President Roosevelt and tried to keep informed of the fighting taking place around the world. Whenever the *Muscatine Journal* arrived, the boys pored over it to absorb and follow the war stories covered in the newspaper. Helene was frightened by the news of the war as she could not comprehend where the fighting was taking place. She was afraid the war would spread to the mainland of the United States and their home might be invaded. She dreaded hearing the radio reports because the news made her feel scared and anxious.

In spite of World War II, one yearly event which continued was the county fair in West Liberty. Held annually in

August, the fair was a major event for both town and country dwellers. Occasionally, Mother took the younger kids to the fair with Jessie and her son, Larry. In addition to the livestock and produce exhibits, the fair featured food vendors and carnival rides. The merry-go-round was always spectacular to see with its bright lights and pretty, painted horses moving up and down to the sound of music. Helene and Jeanne were told they could ride on the fancy carousel, but on one condition which Mother made clear, "I'll buy you girls a ticket, but I want you to sit on the bench." The girls, who were twelve and fourteen, were certainly old enough to hold on to a horse without falling off. But Mother was cautious and the only way they were allowed to ride was to sit together on the stationary bench. Embarrassed and feeling out of place, they sat quietly with somber faces while the pretty horses around them glided along to the music.

Mother used to give each of the girls a few pennies to buy a trinket or to try and win a prize at the fair. It was a big decision where to spend this money, but they ended up with a small toy or necklace sold at a vendor's stand. A taste of cotton candy or fresh lemonade was a special treat as well. It was always a fun day to go to the county fair as there were many sights to see and enjoy.

The Rural Electric Cooperative (REC) expanded their services for rural communities in 1942. Shortly after, the

Porters had their house and outbuildings wired for electricity. This was a drastic improvement in living. No longer were they dependent on kerosene lanterns to help them see in the dark. The kids were fascinated by the light switch and turned the lights off and on in amazement. After the house was wired, Lee installed indoor plumbing. It was a gift to have running water for cooking, bathing, washing and indoor toilets. The new conveniences greatly helped Mother with her daily work in the house.

Helene started attending school at Nichols in eighth grade while Jim started to school there in third grade. Jeanne, Warren and Jane were all attending Nichols High School in 1943. Jane was involved in several plays during high school including her senior class play, *The Poor Fish*. She played the role of the temperamental wife, Mrs. Sylvester Fish, Sr., in this amusing comedy of mistaken identities. While in high school, Jane also played basketball as a forward on the girls' basketball team. She worked part-time at Kirchner's store after school and on Saturdays, making enough money to buy her own clothes for school.

There were some weekends when Jane would have a girlfriend over on Friday night. When Saturday morning came, Jane would not be interested in working at Kirchner's store. Instead, she feigned an illness and her friend would call the store for her saying, "Hello? Mary Jane has the flu today so she will not be able to work." Surprisingly the manager and even Mother tolerated her occasional truancy.

Nichols High School 1944

Mother did well to ensure that each of her children would graduate from high school and was able to buy them all a class ring. She also had their senior pictures taken at a portrait studio in Davenport, Iowa. Jane graduated in 1944 followed by Warren in 1945 and Jeanne in 1946. There were fifteen seniors in Jane's graduating class. One of her friends, Gloria Barber, stayed with the Porters during her senior year when Gloria's family moved out of town. Mother agreed to let her stay so that she could finish her senior year at Nichols. Gloria was a talented basketball player on the same team with Jane. It always seemed as though Mother could make room for one more person at the table.

To Mother's credit, she was able to cash flow the farm successfully under Lee's direction. She stayed focused and used common sense when solving problems. Some of her wise comments included: "Your legs are younger than mine," "He's crazier than a pet coon," "I wouldn't believe him more than a man on the moon," "He doesn't know beans from applesauce," "It's not worth a hill of beans," and "He's a little wet behind the ears," when referring to someone who is inexperienced but thinks he or she has all the answers.

9

HOLDING IT TOGETHER

THE PORTERS were diversified farmers producing melons, potatoes, corn, oats and alfalfa. Additionally, Raymond purchased twenty gilts from a farmer he worked for and began raising hogs. They farrowed in the spring, summer and fall and he sold the hogs in the winter. Raising hogs meant there was a source of meat readily available for the family to consume.

Another venture the Porters became involved with was the purchase of milk cows to produce and sell bottled milk on a route in Nichols. Mother bought the small herd of dairy cows from a farmer who lived close to "Sand 60." The family herded the cows themselves down the road from their current farm location. The cows were tame so the cattle drive went well. Mother, Raymond and Jeanne milked the cows by hand each morning and night. Helene was in charge of the milk house and washed the glass milk bottles. The bottles were quart and pint-sized. A capping machine capped each bottle with a cardboard cap.

Helene, Jeanne, Raymond and Jim by milk house

The milk was delivered by Jeanne and Helene each morning before school. Jeanne would drive the Model T and frequently they would be tardy for school as she was in no hurry to get there. Sometimes they would pick up their friend Louise to ride with them. The ride could be bumpy and rough with Jeanne as the driver, and several bottles were broken along the route. Not realizing that this was the reason why bottles were disappearing Mother said, "I'm going to have to charge the customers for those bottles they aren't returning." When the girls would arrive late to school, the superintendent, Mr. Hedeman, would scold them for being late. Jeanne would be amused by it all and was never worried. She could "pull the wool over his eyes," as Mother used to say.

The milk route provided a significant source of cash income for Mother and it was a wise investment for her. Once again, she was prudent and made good business decisions. The family had their own meat, eggs, milk, cream and butter along with plenty of vegetables, melons and strawberries in the summer. Staples like coffee and sugar were rationed, but the family qualified for large quantities.

After Jane graduated from Nichols High School in 1944, she worked away from home at several jobs. During World II, she worked for a period of time in Middleton, Iowa near Burlington at a major production facility for the United

States military. Jane worked in the ammunitions plant and was well paid. She was one of many American women to work in military arms production during World War II. Jane had an apartment and took the bus to and from home on weekends. In fact, she used some of her money to buy Mother a bedroom set.

During World War II, long troop trains stopped in Nichols for coal and water to supply the steam engines. Churches and the lodge of which Mother was a member, made cookies and cakes, giving them to service men while the train stopped.

Willy was drafted into the United States Army while the war was active. He was stationed on the island of New Guinea in the Pacific Ocean. When he was discharged, he came home with impetigo and some of the girls contracted it. Mother decided it was time for him to leave home and told him he could no longer stay with the family. Hence, that was when they parted.

Warren was set to graduate in 1945. While attending high school in Nichols, he was active on the basketball and baseball teams. A left handed shooter, his height was an asset to the team. In the spring of his senior year, Warren became ill with a severe sore throat. With no antibiotics available, the infection made him very sick. His throat was so swollen he could hardly swallow saliva yet alone eat.

Finally, Doc Moench lanced the abscess so it could drain and heal. Warren lost several pounds and was very thin, weighing only one hundred and forty-one pounds when he underwent his physical for the service. Since Warren had taken extra subjects, he was eligible to graduate from high school after Christmas during his senior year. To avoid being drafted in February of 1945, when he turned eighteen, he opted to voluntarily enlist in the United States Navy.

In the spring of 1945, both Lee and Warren enlisted in the Navy. Mother was nervous about them serving, but she held back her reservations and let them go. Raymond took over the management of the farming operation in Lee's absence. Jeanne and Jim also helped by driving the tractor and assisting with chores. As a family, they were able to maintain the farming operation while Lee and Warren served their country.

Lee joined with long-time friend, Doug Stevenson, who had originally persuaded him to enlist in the Army. Lee and Doug were to report for duty in St. Louis, Missouri. Upon their arrival, they saw two signs posted which read, Navy and Army. It was at this point that Lee changed his mind to join the Navy, even though his friend Doug chose to serve in the Army. That was the last time Lee saw his friend as they lost contact with each other.

Unknown to either of them, Lee and Warren would be sent to the same boot camp at Great Lakes Naval Base near Chicago. They were eating their meals one day when they happened to look up and see each other. Warren had thought Lee was in the Army so it was a surprise to discover they were in naval training together. Following boot camp they came home on leave in May of 1945 and waited for their assignments.

The family with Lee and Warren in May 1945

Lee was assigned as a crew member on an LST (Tank Landing Ship) when the United States was planning an invasion of Japan. His ship was docked in Seattle being repaired and fitted to be loaded on a transport carrier sailing to Japan. Fortunately, the war ended in August 1945 so that mission was aborted. Lee's crew was split up and he was assigned to a rescue and salvage ship in Pearl Harbor. This is where he spent the remainder of his time in service, serving a total of thirteen months from the time he enlisted.

Lee in Hawaii in 1945

126

Mother wrote to both Lee and Warren, updating them on the farming operation and local news from Nichols. Mother always read the comic strip, *Boots and Her Buddies*, in the *Muscatine Journal*. One of the most notable strips was when Boots got married. Mother saved this, clipped it out and sent it to Lee.

Warren served on a ship named, USS *Bunker Hill*. When it came in to dock in Bremerton, Washington, it had been hit by suicide planes in the war. He spent two months in Bremerton before setting sail later to Hawaii and then to Japan on a military cargo ship. Both Warren and Lee served until April 1946 when they were discharged.

Mother followed the news of the war by listening to the radio. With two sons serving in the military, she was intent on staying informed of the latest developments. It was a shock to hear in August of 1945 that atomic bombs had been dropped on Japan, but Mother had trust in President Truman and hoped that these bombings would lead to its surrender.

When World War II finally ended, it was a victory celebrated all over the country, including the town of Nichols. The fire siren in Nichols sounded and church and school bells rang. The news of the war ending spread on the party telephone lines as well. At home, Mother was elated to hear the news on the radio. She was so relieved to learn that the war was over. It did not worry her that Lee and Warren were still serving in the military because she knew they were safer, now that the war had come to an end.

In the fall of 1945, Warren came home on a short leave from the Navy. Duck hunting season was open and he took Jim with him to hunt. Jim had never been duck hunting before. Warren used a duck call to attract a flock of Mallards that landed near their decoys. He told Jim to shoot first and Jim got two ducks with one shot. Warren shot several more while they were flying. Jim used an old, single shot twelve gauge shotgun. In his excitement, he did not realize at first how bad the recoil was. His shoulder was tender and sore the next few days. But it did not seem to bother him as that was the first time he shot a duck and was thrilled.

Mother on the farm in 1945

After Lee was discharged, he returned home to manage the family farm. Raymond, then, started a feed business and sold livestock feed in Nichols. Warren also worked at his feed store after being discharged from service. It was a relief to have them both home and the farm continued to operate soundly, just as it had during the war under Mother's wise management.

Porter House, March 1948

10

FAMILY TIES AND NEW BEGINNINGS

DURING THE LATE 1940s, the family adjusted to changes which occurred when the siblings graduated from high school, started new jobs or got married. Mother and Lee continued to manage the family farm while Raymond moved to Nichols to start his feed business with the help of Warren. Jane worked at the telephone office in Iowa City then later got married. Jessie and Larry moved to Muscatine where Jessie found employment.

As part of Raymond's feed sales, he won a sales contest and was awarded two purebred Labrador Retrievers. One of the dogs was black and the other a golden color. He gave them to the family so they could have freedom living on a farm. Jim enjoyed taking them hunting. The golden colored dog, Champ, was his favorite. Sometimes on Sunday mornings, Jim would help Mother catch a chicken for dinner. Mother only had to point at the chicken she wanted and Champ caught the bird and fetched it. He had a very soft mouth and never left a mark on any bird.

Attending dances was a favorite pastime of the family even if it meant driving thirty miles. On Sunday nights, dances were held at the ballroom in Stockton, Iowa. The Porters and their friends looked forward to going, and Lee's car was filled to capacity when he drove this lively group of young adults to Stockton. It was always late when they returned home and not easy to wake up on time for school the next morning. Circle dances were popular at these events and everyone enjoyed the night.

Another dance hall was in Nichols above Mills' service station. Several local bands played and even some well known names from bigger cities like Leo Greco. The crowds were large when popular bands played. The structure of the hall was questionable as the floor felt like it was heaving when big crowds danced. But it was a fun place to go to swing dance to the music.

In the spring of 1946, Jeanne graduated from Nichols High School. She was a gifted athlete in school, playing very well in basketball with a strong hook shot. At that time there was no limit on how long a player could be inside the box beneath the basket. Jeanne was taller than the other girls and could easily grab the ball and hook it in for a basket. She continued to drive the car to deliver the milk in the mornings on the milk route with Helene and their friend, Louise. Following her graduation from high school, Jeanne became engaged and then left home after getting married.

Mother became more involved in social organizations during this time as well. She often attended women's church meetings at the Nichols Methodist Church. She was known for bringing her sweet potato pie to potlucks and dinners. Mother and the girls enjoyed attending services on Sundays at the Methodist Church.

Helene graduated from Nichols High School in 1949. She, too, was active in basketball and played the clarinet in the school band. As a senior, her class took an organized trip for Senior Skip Day to Dubuque, Iowa. Helene also worked part-time at Brugman's store in Nichols.

In late 1949, Lee decided to sell the farm and discontinue farming. He and his wife moved shortly after to International Falls, Minnesota to operate a fishing resort. Mother, Warren, Helene and Jim moved to a house in Nichols. Helene helped Mother with painting and making improvements to the house before she left home to get married.

Mother now had even more time for social activities and was actively involved in the women's circle of the Methodist Church in Nichols. She also became a member of the Rebekah Lodge, the female auxiliary association of the Independent Order of the Odd Fellows Lodge. The club sponsored social and charitable activities in the community.

Jim started high school in 1950 at Nichols High School and was active in sports. He played basketball and also baseball where he was a pitcher for the team. Jim also helped Raymond in his feed business working for him part-time. After school and on Saturdays Jim helped mix and sack feed, and he also delivered orders to farmers. He appreciated having the job because it gave him spending money.

During Jim's junior year in high school, he worked part-time for Max Hanft at a garage and gas station. Jim worked before and after school and on Saturdays pumping gas, washing cars and fixing flat tires. He was grateful for the opportunity and learned a great deal from Max on developing a good attitude. Max was a good role model for Jim.

Jim bought a 1930 Model A Ford while he was a junior in high school. One Sunday afternoon during the winter, Jim and his friends from school had an ice skating party on a nearby lake. Jim decided to drive his Model A onto the frozen lake and pull his friends on the ice with the car. The third time around the lake the ice started to crack and the car fell through. Water was up to the bottom of the doors and Jim had to climb out the window of the car to escape. The car was almost fifty yards from shore.

A friend of Jim's went to get his dad's tractor. Jim and his friends chopped ice all the way to shore so a rope could be tied onto the car to pull it out with the tractor. They were able to get the car out of the lake and Jim drove it home. But the next morning when Jim started it, he could not get it to move. Water had seeped into the differential and froze. Jim told Max Hanft what had happened so Max brought the car down to his garage to thaw out and drain the differential.

Jim was afraid to tell Mother about the incident, but he decided he should be honest with her. Mother was certainly not pleased and voiced her displeasure. "What did you expect? Did you really think that car could drive on water?"

Jim learned his lesson and vowed not to do anything like that again.

Warren bought a new Chevrolet car and occasionally let Jim borrow it. One Saturday afternoon, Jim was washing and shining up the car along with his shoes. Mother spotted him and asked, "Jim, what do you have up your sleeve?" He told Mother that he and a friend had dates with two girls in Muscatine to take them to a movie. "Well, can't you find any local girls from Nichols to go to a show?" Mother asked. She warned him to be careful when driving in Muscatine. "That city has street lights and people don't always stop at them. You be sure and stop at the red lights and look twice before you start out." Mother was cautious, but wise, and always gave good advice whether they wanted to hear it or not.

Warren had been driving forty miles one way to work at the pork processing plant, Oscar Mayer, in Davenport and came to the conclusion that the drive was too long, especially in the winters. He purchased a house in Davenport and Mother moved there with him in 1953. Jim had a few months left before graduating from high school so he stayed with Raymond and his wife in Nichols. After graduation, Jim joined Mother and Warren in Davenport, working at first for a sheet metal company and then later enlisting in the United States Air Force.

Mother enjoyed living in Davenport and was able to find employment doing several part-time jobs. Her family had all married by 1956 and were now busy with their own children. Later, Mother moved to Muscatine where she shared a house with her daughter-in-law, Jessie. Keeping busy as a cook for a nursing home, Mother enjoyed her life in Muscatine and kept in close contact with her family.

Jessie's son, Larry, had married and also lived in Muscatine with his wife and children. In February 1971, Larry's wife suddenly passed away after suffering a heart attack. The tragic incident left Larry alone with four young children. Mother accompanied Larry to meet with Raymond to discuss burial arrangements. They decided to purchase several plots at the Nichols cemetery in one location where they would someday be buried together as a family. Once again, Mother's strength and leadership in a time of crisis was invaluable as she lent support to Larry during this difficult time.

In making this decision, Mother had also made her final arrangements to be laid to rest in the Nichols cemetery. She desired to be buried close to her surviving family near Nichols. A lasting attribute of Mother was that she made wise decisions, always keeping her family in mind.

Late in 1975, while undergoing a routine physical for her job, Mother was told that a spot was detected on her lung.

Due to concerns that it may have been tuberculosis, Mother was no longer permitted to work in public healthcare as a cook at the nursing home. Not wanting to worry anyone, Mother kept this discovery to herself. It was evident that Mother had something on her mind when she wrote her son, Jim, a letter in the spring of 1976. "Jim, I think it would be a good idea if you and the family came home to visit this summer. It's been awhile and I'd like to see all of you again." Jim had recently retired from the United States Air Force and was living in Spokane, Washington. Without questioning Mother's request, Jim complied with her wishes and later felt so fortunate he and his family came when they did.

On a Sunday evening in September, Jessie called Mother's children who lived close by her and told them they should come right away. Mother was not feeling well. When Helene, Raymond and Jane arrived, they could see that Mother was ill and uncomfortable with pain. They admitted her to the hospital and were then informed for the first time that Mother had lung cancer. Being the strong and courageous woman that she was, Mother had not wanted to worry or burden her family. She had told Jessie, but otherwise refrained from disclosing the news to others.

Devastated by her diagnosis, Mother's children did their best to accommodate her while she underwent radiation treatment at the hospital. They made it a point to bring her home on weekends so she could rest comfortably in her own house. Growing weaker as the days passed by, Mother was later moved to a nursing home facility in West Liberty where family visited her daily.

Close to the end of autumn 1976, three days before Thanksgiving, Mother passed away. Although her family was sad and somber as they grieved over the loss of their beloved Mother, they could not ignore the significance of her passing coinciding with Thanksgiving, a holiday reflective of her life. There was so much to be thankful and grateful for because Mother lived her life for her family. Up to her final days on earth, Mother lived a selfless life focused on those around her. Leaving behind her imprint of strength, courage and wisdom, her spirit would live on and always remain a lasting memory of her remarkable life.

EPILOGUE

LOTTIE PORTER was an extraordinary woman whose strength and courage not only gave her the fortitude to endure challenging times of the Great Depression and the years which followed, but allowed her to keep her family together. Unassuming, but yet strong in spirit, she was resolute and determined to satisfy the needs of her family. This led to the ownership and successful operation of her family's farm. Her wisdom and sound judgment helped her to manage her life and the lives of those she cared for and loved.

When her son, Jim, was serving in the Air Force, he was stationed for a period of time in Alaska. During the summer of 1970, Mother visited Jim and his family. That was the highlight of her life. It was her first experience on an airplane. Mother flew non-stop from Chicago O'Hare International Airport to Anchorage, Alaska. She truly enjoyed her flight and remarked about the mountains she flew over. She loved the ocean, the scenery and the beauty of this magnificent state. Sometimes she just stood in awe, staring at the grandiose mountains. It was a trip she was so deserving of.

On November 22, 1976, at the age of 82, Mother passed away. She always admired John F. Kennedy and would have been touched to know they shared the same date of their passing. Mother was survived by four sons: Lee Ulch, Raymond Porter, Warren Porter, and Jim Porter and three daughters: Mary Jane (Simpson) Ruess, Jeanne Maher and Helene Salemink. In addition, she had twenty-five grandchildren, twelve great-grandchildren and one great-great-grandchild at the time of her death.

It has been an honor to write about my grandmother's life and the lives of her family. I was twelve years old when she passed away and I regret not having known her better. Still, her life lives on through the treasured memories that have been told and re-told over the years. Putting it into perspective made me admire Mother's courage and strength, and I wanted to preserve her authenticity. It is my hope that this book serves that purpose and that those who read it will continue to celebrate Mother's memory and this very important period in American and world history.

Renetta Burlage
July 2009

Lottie Charlotte DeVault 1913

Mother
Lottie Porter circa 1967

NOTES

NOTES

NOTES

NOTES

NOTES

NOTES

NOTES

www.ingramcontent.com/pod-product-compliance
Lightning Source LLC
LaVergne TN
LVHW011234080426
835509LV00005B/486